Public Financial Management Reform in the Middle East and North Africa

An Overview of Regional Experience

Robert P. Beschel Jr.
Mark Ahern

THE WORLD BANK
Washington, D.C.

© 2012 International Bank for Reconstruction and Development / International Development Association or
The World Bank
1818 H Street NW
Washington DC 20433
Telephone: 202-473-1000
Internet: www.worldbank.org

1 2 3 4   15 14 13 12

World Bank Studies are published to communicate the results of the Bank's work to the development community with the least possible delay. The manuscript of this paper therefore has not been prepared in accordance with the procedures appropriate to formally-edited texts.

This volume is a product of the staff of The World Bank with external contributions. The findings, interpretations, and conclusions expressed in this volume do not necessarily reflect the views of The World Bank, its Board of Executive Directors, or the governments they represent.

The World Bank does not guarantee the accuracy of the data included in this work. The boundaries, colors, denominations, and other information shown on any map in this work do not imply any judgment on the part of The World Bank concerning the legal status of any territory or the endorsement or acceptance of such boundaries.

Rights and Permissions

The material in this work is subject to copyright. Because The World Bank encourages dissemination of its knowledge, this work may be reproduced, in whole or in part, for noncommercial purposes as long as full attribution to the work is given.

For permission to reproduce any part of this work for commercial purposes, please send a request with complete information to the Copyright Clearance Center Inc., 222 Rosewood Drive, Danvers, MA 01923, USA; telephone: 978-750-8400; fax: 978-750-4470; Internet: www.copyright.com.

All other queries on rights and licenses, including subsidiary rights, should be addressed to the Office of the Publisher, The World Bank, 1818 H Street NW, Washington, DC 20433, USA; fax: 202-522-2422; e-mail: pubrights@worldbank.org.

ISBN (paper): 978-0-8213-9529-5
ISBN (electronic): 978-0-8213-9530-1
DOI: 10.1596/978-0-8213-9529-5

Cover image by Marsi Pandolf Beschel, used with permission.

Library of Congress Cataloging-in-Publication Data

Ahern, Mark E.
   Public financial management reform in the Middle East and North Africa : an overview of regional experience / [Mark E. Ahern, Robert P. Beschel, Jr.]
        p. cm.
   "Part I, Overview and summary, June 2010."
   ISBN 978-0-8213-9529-5 -- ISBN 978-0-8213-9530-1
   1. Finance, Public--Africa, North. 2. Finance, Public--Middle East. I. Beschel, Robert P. II. World Bank. III. Title.
   HJ1451.A44 2012
   352.4'23670956--dc23

                                                                          2012010606

Contents

Boxes

Figures

Tables

Acknowledgments

We would like to gratefully acknowledge the assistance of many who contributed to this report. The first are the individual chapter authors, without whose insights, hard work, and diligence it would not have been possible. They include Arun Arya, David Biggs, Robert Bou Jaoude, Elena Moraciella, David Shand, and Daniel Tommasi. We would also like to thank a number of Lead and Senior Country Economists and Public Sector Specialists who provided valuable inputs and insights along the way, including Sebnem Akkaya, Jorge Araujo, Sherine el-Shawarby, Ndiame Diop, Khalid el Massnaoui, Santiago Herrera, Catherine Laurent, Jose Lopez-Calix, Stefano Paternostro, and Yahia Khairi Said. Guenter Heidenhof provided valuable inputs and support at various stages of the preparation process. Stephen MacLeod provided inputs into the early stages of this effort.

Nithya Nagarajan drafted more detailed case studies of the tax, customs, and public financial management reforms in the Arab Republic of Egypt and the West Bank and Gaza, assisted in the case of Egypt by Andrew H.W. Stone. These cases are part of a broader collaborative effort to identify and document promising examples of public sector reform throughout the Middle East and North Africa region, which is run jointly by the World Bank and the Dubai School of Government.

The peer reviewers included Richard Allen of the IMF's Fiscal Affairs Department, James Brumby, and Salvatore Schiavo-Campo. We are grateful for the excellent research assistants who helped collect and analyze the data and prepare the final report, including Lida Bteddini, Lydia Habhab, and Hala Hanna. Mavo Ranaivoarivelo helped in compiling the final document. Finally, we would like to thank Alex Sperling for providing logistical and organizational support with her usual grace, charm, and efficiency. We wish her well in her new assignment with the Bank's Legal Department.

Support for this report came from the Norwegian Governance Trust Fund and Governance Scale-Up Funds from the Middle East and North Africa Vice Presidency. Additional support for a number of the Public Expenditure and Financial Accountability (PEFA) exercises came from the European Union, including Morocco and Tunisia. The Jordan PEFA exercise was entirely funded and conducted by the European Union.

This report is dedicated to the memory of John Wetter, our colleague who worked extensively on issues of macroeconomic stability, fiscal sustainability, and public financial management in a number of countries throughout the Levant. His wit, wisdom, and humor are missed.

Mark E. Ahern
Robert P. Beschel Jr.

About the Authors

Mark Ahern joined the Middle East and North Africa Region of the World Bank in July 2008 as a Governance Advisor. The main focus of his work is on public financial management (PFM) issues where he has been most involved with reforms in West Bank and Gaza, and the Syrian Arab Republic. In early 2012, he left MENA for the East Asia Pacific Region of the Bank and currently is Lead Public Sector Specialist supporting PFM reforms in Indonesia. Before joining the World Bank, he worked for the International Monetary Fund (IMF) for eight years, where he was a resident PFM advisor in various countries in Africa, the former Soviet Union, and the Middle East. He was also involved in a large number of technical assistance missions on PFM issues.

From 2004 to 2008, Mr. Ahern was based in the IMFs Middle East technical assistance center in Beirut (METAC), where he worked as the PFM advisor for 10 countries in the Middle East region. He is originally from New Zealand and started his career by spending 15 years with the New Zealand Treasury working on sectoral policy issues, tax policy, and budget management. In his budget management role, he spent three years as Budget Director. Mr. Ahern has an MA in Economics from Canterbury University in New Zealand.

Robert P. Beschel Jr. is on an external service assignment from the World Bank. In 2010, he was recruited by the Office of Tony Blair and the Government of Kuwait to serve as Deputy Director for Policy (and currently Acting Director for the Policy Unit) in the newly created Technical and Advisory Office (TAO) of the Prime Minister. Previously, he was responsible for coordinating the Bank's work on governance and public management throughout the MENA region and worked closely with senior officials to help realize their reform agendas. He sat on the World Bank's Public Sector Governance Board, which manages the Bank's global work on governance and public management, and is a core member of the Bank's Global Expert Team on Enhancing Public Sector Performance. He is also a member of the Bank's civil service, anticorruption, and e-governance thematic groups.

Previously, Mr. Beschel was Lead Public Sector Specialist in the World Bank's South Asia Vice Presidency. From 1996–99, he served as Strategy and Policy Officer at the Asian Development Bank (ADB) in Manila, where he was the principal author of the ADB's anticorruption policy (which was approved unanimously by the Board in July 1997) and Vice President of the ADB Staff Council. He has served as a long-term consultant to the World Bank Institute and as Executive Director of Project Liberty, a major initiative of Harvard's Kennedy School of Government to promote public sector reform in economies in transition. He has also served as Special Assistant for International Affairs to the president of the Carnegie Corporation of New York.

Dr. Beschel has an MA in Public Administration from Harvard University's John F. Kennedy School of Government and an MA and PhD in Political Science from Harvard's Government Department.

Arun Arya is the World Bank's field-based Governance Adviser in the Republic of Yemen since 2006. He is leading the Bank's Public Sector and Governance Program including, Public Finance Management and Anti-Corruption. During his tenure in the Republic of Yemen, he has assisted the government in conducting the Public Expenditure and Financial Accountability (PEFA) Assessment and in developing the second phase of the National Public Finance Management Reform Action Plan. Mr. Arya has also led the Bank's Anti-Corruption program and has provided technical assistance to the government in conducting the National Survey on Corruption, a Diagnostic Review on Anti-Corruption Legal and Regulatory Framework, the Development of National Anti-Corruption Strategy, and Building Civil Society Coalition against Corruption.

Prior to joining the Bank, Mr. Arya worked for the Danish aid agency DANIDA as the Senior Sector Adviser for Water and Sanitation sector in Bangladesh, where he assisted the Government in preparing the Sector Development Program. He has also worked for the Indian Administrative Service (IAS) for 19 years, in which he developed wide ranging experience in governance, the administration of justice, economic development, social development, electoral administration, conflict management, media management, and human rights. He completed a BA (Honors) in Economics from the St. Stephen's College, Delhi University, and has a post graduate degree in Management from the Indian Institute of Management in Ahmedabad, India.

David F. Biggs is currently working as a consultant on PFM issues. Previously, he was a Senior Public Sector Specialist in the World Bank's MENA Region. In this capacity, he was primarily responsible for coordinating the Bank's work on governance in Iraq and its PFM practice throughout the MENA region. He worked closely with senior officials in partner governments to help realize their PFM reform goals. His main focal countries were Iraq and Egypt.

Prior to joining the World Bank in 2006, Mr. Biggs was a Senior Governance Adviser in the British Government's Department for International Development (DFID) for almost eight years. During that period, he was responsible at various times for DFID's governance work in Latin America and the Caribbean, Eastern Europe and Central Asia, and the United Kingdom's Overseas Territories. He also worked as Head of the Public Financial Management and Accountability team in DFID's Policy Division and the Asia Policy Directorate in London.

Mr. Biggs has a BA in Social Studies (Economic History) from Exeter University in the United Kingdom. He has been a Certified Public Finance Accountant (CPFA) since 1973, and was a senior employee of the awarding body, the UK's Chartered Institute of Public Finance and Accountancy (CIPFA), for 10 years. He has worked on PFM issues for 40 years in the United Kingdom and a large number of overseas countries, including 3–4 year assignments in Kenya and Zimbabwe.

Robert Bou Jaoude is currently a Senior Financial Management Specialist at the World Bank. His experience covers Lebanon, Syria, the Islamic Republic of Iran, Iraq, Jordan, Egypt, and Kuwait. He has led a number of high-profile analytic and capacity building activities in PFM and corporate financial reporting. He has also advised governments in different areas of financial management in medium income and post conflict countries, including support to Lebanon for the establishment of a reporting system on extra budgetary activities financing post war reconstruction. He is also a Member of the Quality and Result Committee providing advice to the Financial Management sector board on Financial Management and Quality issues.

Prior to joining the Bank, as a member of the United Nations Development Programme (UNPD) team, Mr. Bou Jaoude provided advice and support to the Lebanese government in its reform program. He led the work on the trade facilitation and provided advice in the areas of budget reforms and the internal control environment at the Ministry of Finance.

During his career, Mr. Bou Jaoude gained professional experience in Lebanon, Canada, and Jordan. He is a Certified Management Accountant and a graduate of McGill University in Canada. He also holds an MA in money and banking and a BA in Finance and Accounting from the American University of Beirut. He started his professional experience upon graduation in 1983 and has gained more than 22 years of diversified professional experience in the banking, private and public sectors, in addition to working with the UNDP. His experience covers accounting, auditing, financial controls, treasury operations, retail financial, banking operations, banking supervision and regulation.

Elena Morachiello is currently a Consultant on Public Financial Management issues. She mostly works with the Middle East and North Africa Financial Management Network (MNAFM) at the World Bank on a range of countries such as Lebanon, Egypt, Jordan, Iraq, and the West Bank and Gaza. She also participated in the 2008 Uganda PEFA Assessment.

Between early 2004 and early 2008, she worked at the Audit Commission for the European Space Agency in Paris, especially on budgetary issues, including medium-term planning, budget transparency and classification, cost-accounting and activity based budgeting. She also assessed the transition to accrual accounting and to full alignment with the International Public Sector Accounting Standards (IPSAS). In Paris, she attended Organisation for Economic Co-operation and Development (OECD) public sector accruals symposiums and the meetings of the Working Party of Senior Budget Officials (SBO). Between 1999 and 2004, she was a World Bank Consultant for the Middle East and North Africa Economic Policy division (MNSED), focusing on Public Expenditure Reviews, including the assessment of contingent liabilities, extra-budgetary practices and quasi-fiscal activities.

Ms. Morachiello earned a BS (Economics) from the London School of Economics and Political Science in London; an MA from the Institut d'Etudes Politiques in Paris; and an MA in International Economics from the School of Advanced International Studies in Washington, DC. She has published articles on development issues for *Il Sole 24 Ore*, Italy's leading financial daily.

David Shand retired from the World Bank in 2005 but continues working as a consultant on PFM issues. He joined the Bank in 1998 as a Senior Public Sector Specialist at the World Bank Institute before transferring to the East Asia and Pacific region. He then spent four years as Financial Management Advisor in OPCS, including six months as acting head of the Bank's financial management network. He has extensive experience in PFM work as task manager of a number of Public Expenditure Reviews (PERs) and Country Financial Accountability Assessments (CFAAs) in various regions. In 2005, he chaired the OECD/Development Assistance Committee (DAC) task force on PFM and played a significant role in the development of the PEFA analysis.

In the MENA region he managed the 2004 West Bank and Gaza CFAA and was a major contributor to the West Bank and Gaza 2007 PER, which included a PEFA analysis. He also wrote the PFM chapter of the 2005 Egypt PER and has also contributed to training courses for Iraqi officials.

Before joining the Bank, Mr. Shand was a PFM consultant in the Fiscal Affairs Department of IMF and worked for four years in the OECD on public sector management reform. Prior to that, he held senior positions in the federal and state governments of Australia, including Deputy Secretary of the Victorian Treasury and Queensland Public Service Commissioner. He also taught public sector accounting and finance at the Australian National University and Victoria University of Wellington, New Zealand. Mr. Shand holds dual New Zealand and Australian nationality. He currently resides in Auckland, New Zealand. He is a graduate in accounting and economics from Victoria University of Wellington and is a Fellow of the Australian Society of CPAs.

Daniel Tommasi is an international consultant in the areas of fiscal policy, public expenditure management, and macroeconomic management. He has worked as an adviser to governments and consultant for international organizations, including the World Bank, the International Monetary Fund, the European Commission, and the Asian Development Bank. He has worked for over 30 years in some 40 countries in Africa, Asia, the Caribbean, Central and Eastern Europe, and the Pacific Islands.

His experience includes technical assistance in implementing budgetary reforms, public expenditure programming, debt management, and preparing economic strategy and fiscal policy. He has frequently provided training to government officials in the area of public finance. He is currently providing training to the European Commission officials in PFM. He has participated in the preparation, negotiation, and supervision of several programs supported by the IMF and the World Bank, either as a consultant for the World Bank or as an advisor for various governments. He has participated in several public expenditure reviews and public expenditure management assessments for international organizations.

Mr. Tommasi is the author of several papers on expenditure management and the co-author of two manuals: *Managing Government Expenditure*, published by the Asian Development Bank in 1999; and *Managing Public Expenditure: A Reference Book for Transition Countries*, published by the OECD in 2001.

Acronyms and Abbreviations

ACCT	Treasury Central Accounting Unit (Algeria)
AfDB	African Development Bank
AFMIS	Accounting-based Financial Management System
AGES	Automated Government Expenditure System
AP	Autorisations de Programme
ARABOSAI	Arab Organization of Supreme Audit Institutions
ASOSAI	Asian Organization of Supreme Audit Institutions
BCC	Budget Call Circular
BdL	Central Bank of Lebanon
BSA	Board of Supreme Audit (Iraq)
BSMP	Budget System Modernization Project (Algeria)
CACI	Central Inspection Agency (Syria)
CAO	Compliance Advisor Ombudsman
CBE	Central Bank of Egypt
CBI	Central Bank of Iraq
CBY	Central Bank of the Republic of Yemen
CDR	Council for Development and Reconstruction
CFAA	Country Financial Accountability Assessment
CGED	General Control of Expenditures Commitment
CGSP	Public Services Audit Office (Tunisia)
CIB	Central Inspection Board (Lebanon)
CMU	Cash Management Unit
CNED	National Fund of Equipment for Development
CoA	Chart of Accounts (Jordan)/Court of Accounts (Lebanon)
COCA	Central Organization of Control and Audit (the Republic of Yemen)
COFC	Central Organization for Financial Control (Syria)
COFOG	Classification of the Functions of Government
COG	Central Government
COI	Commission of Integrity (Iraq)
COR	Council of Representatives (Iraq)
CP	Credits de Paiement
CPA	Coalition Provisional Authority (Iraq)
CPAR	Country Procurement Assessment Report
CPI	Corruption Perception Index
CPIA	Country Policy and Institutional Assessment
CSMP	Civil Service Modernization Project (the Republic of Yemen)
CST	Central Sales Tax
DA	Algerian Dinar
DB	Budget Directorate
DFID	Department for International Development (United Kingdom)
DGCP	General Directorate for Public Accounting (Tunisia)

DMFAS	Debt Management Financial Analysis System
DPL	Development Policy Loan
DPM	Deputy Prime Minister
DPPR	Development Plan for Poverty Reduction
DPR	Detailed Project Report
EC	European Commission
EdL	Electricité du Liban
EFMIS	Emergency Fiscal Management Reform Implementation Support
ESW	Economic and Sector Work
EU	European Union
FAD	Fiscal Affairs Department
FE	Forward Estimate
FMIS	Financial Management Information Systems
FRR	Revenue Regulation Fund (Algeria)
FY	Fiscal Year
GBD	General Budget Directorate (Jordan)
GBO	Budget Management by Objectives (Tunisia)
GCC	Gulf Cooperation Council
GCF	Financial Audit Office (Tunisia)
GDDS	Government Data Dissemination Standard
GDP	Gross Domestic Product
GFSM	Government Finance Statistics Manual
GFMIS	Government Financial Management Information System
GFS/COFOG	Government Finance Statistics/Classification of the Function of Government
GID	Integrated Expenditure Control System
GoE	Government of Egypt
GoI	Government of Iraq
GoJ	Government of Jordan
GoL	Government of Lebanon
GoY	Government of the Republic of Yemen
GPC	General Party Congress (the Republic of Yemen)
GTZ	German Technical Cooperation
GU	Governmental Unit
HCCAF	High Commission for Administrative and Financial Audit (Tunisia)
HIPC	Heavily Indebted Poor Countries
HRC	Higher Relief Commission (Lebanon)
ICI	International Compact for Iraq
ICR	Implementation Completion Report
ICRG	International Country Risk Guide
ID	Iraqi Dinar
IDA	International Development Association
IDF	Institutional Development Fund
IFMCA	Institutional Financial Management Capacity Assessments
IFMIS	Iraq Financial Management Information System
IGF	Inspectorate-General of Finance

IMF	International Monetary Fund
INTOSAI	International Organization of Supreme Audit Institutions
IPSAS	International Public Sector Accounting Standards
ISDT	Income and Sales Tax Department
ITD	Income Tax Department
ITF	Iraq Trust Fund
JD	Jordan Dinar
KRG	Kurdistan Regional Government (Iraq)
LOLF	Loi Organique Relative aux Lois de Finances (Morocco)
LTO	Large Taxpayer Office
MDCI	Ministry of Development and International Cooperation (Tunisia)
MDG	Millennium Development Goals
MED	Ministry of Economic Development
MEF	Ministry of Economy and Finance (Morocco)
MENA	Middle East and North Africa
METAC	Middle East Regional Technical Assistance Center
MMSP	Ministry of Public Sector Modernization (Morocco)
MOF	Ministry of Finance
MOH	Ministry of Health
MOLA	Ministry of Local Administration (the Republic of Yemen)
MOP	Ministry of Planning
MOPDC	Ministry of Planning and Development Cooperation (Iraq)
MOPIC	Ministry of Planning and International Cooperation
MSAD	Ministry of State of Administrative Development (Egypt)
MTBF	Medium Term Budget Framework
MTEF	Medium Term Expenditure Framework
MTFF	Medium Term Fiscal Framework
MTO	Medium Taxpayer Office
NFTI	National Fiscal Training Institute
NGO	Nongovernmental Organization
NRA	National Reform Agenda
NSSF	National Social Security Fund
OBL	Organic Budget Law
ODPM	Office of the Deputy Prime Minister
OECD	Organization for Economic Cooperation and Development
OPM	Office of the Prime Minister
PA	Palestinian Authority
PAL	Public Accounting Law (Lebanon)
PARL	Public Administration Reform Loan
PARP	Public Administration Reform Program
PCSC	Complementary Plan for Support to Growth (Algeria)
PDD	Public Debt Department
PEFA	Public Expenditure and Financial Accountability
PEIA	Public Expenditure and Institutional Assessment
PEM-TA	Public Expenditure Management—Technical Assistance
PER	Public Expenditure Review

PFM	Public Financial Management
PFMAU	Public Financial Management Advisory Unit
PIF	Palestinian Investment Fund
PIU	Project Implementation Unit
PLC	Palestinian Legislative Council
PPP	Purchasing Power Parity
PRDP	Preparation of a Development Plan
PSA	Production Share Agreement
PSR	Public Sector Reform
ROB	Results-Oriented Budgeting
ROSC	Report on the Observance of Standards and Codes
SAACB	State Audit and Administrative Control Bureau (West Bank and Gaza)
SAI	Supreme Audit Institutions
SDDS	Special Data Dissemination Standards
SIGIR	Special Inspector General for Iraqi Reconstruction
SOE	State-Owned Enterprise
SONATRACH	Société Nationale pour la Recherche, la Production, le Transport, la Transformation, et la Commercialisation des Hydrocarbures s.p.a. (Algeria)
SNG	Subnational Government
SPC	Special Planning Commission (Syria)
STA	Special Treasury Account
STD	Sales Tax Department
SU	Spending Units
TGR	Kingdom General Treasury (Morocco)
TSA	Treasury Single Account (Egypt)
UNCAC	United Nations Convention Against Corruption
UNDP	United Nations Development Program
USAID	United States Agency for International Development
VAT	Value Added Tax
WBG	West Bank and Gaza
WGI	World Governance Indicators
YER	Yemeni Riyal

PART I

Overview and Summary

Executive Summary

Introduction

One of the most important functions governments perform is that of mobilizing and deploying financial resources to achieve their objectives. According to the most recent World Bank data, governments throughout the Middle East and North Africa (MENA) region spent approximately US$407 billion dollars in 2007 in delivering their policy, regulatory and service functions. The way in which this money is spent has huge implications for their broader development trajectory. For example, a one percent efficiency gain in the Arab Republic of Egypt's budget for 2009 would yield US$637 million dollars—enough resources to build 40,000 schools, pave 4,500 kilometers of highway, or recruit an additional 600,000 doctors. It is therefore not surprising that issues of public financial management, or PFM, have been at the heart of governance reform programs in virtually all of the economies in the region.

For governments to perform their spending function well, their PFM practices should meet certain well-established criteria. Government spending should be affordable, in that it takes place within a framework that ensures expenditure is consistent with monetary and fiscal policy objectives and sustainable in the long term. Governments should optimize the allocation of public resources between different sectors and expenditure categories in a way that reflects their policy priorities, including sustainable growth as well as human and social development. Such expenditure should be efficient, in that it maximizes output for a given set of inputs, and effective, in that it supports the successful realization of the government's goals. It should also be transparent; conducted in accordance with the relevant laws and regulations; and undertaken with appropriate checks and balances to ensure financial probity.

While such objectives are relatively straightforward, their realization can be anything but. In many MENA economies, PFM reforms have been on the agenda for a decade or more. This report seeks to reflect upon this experience to date and better understand the nature of the PFM challenges confronting these economies. This study surveys these reforms across 10 Arab economies: Algeria, Egypt, Iraq, Jordan, Lebanon, Morocco, the Syrian Arab Republic, Tunisia, the West Bank and Gaza and the Republic of Yemen. They were selected partly because they are places where the Bank has been heavily engaged on PFM issues and been able to gather a wealth of comparative information. They also represent an interesting cross-section of administrative traditions and different levels of development. At the high end, in 2007 Lebanon had a GDP per capita of US$6,017 and a life expectancy of 72 years, whereas at the other end of the spectrum, these figures stand at US$973 and 62 years for the Republic of Yemen. Lebanon has around 38.3 internet users per 1,000 citizens, as opposed to only 0.9 for Iraq. Taken together, these economies are home to over two thirds of MENA's population and nearly one third of its GDP. Many of the findings from this analysis will be of relevance to other MENA economies as well.

Turning to the substance of PFM reforms, the study considers to what extent these economies dealing are with common problems stemming from similar administrative traditions and comparable levels of development, or unique challenges grounded within their own particular historical or bureaucratic experience. The analysis also seeks to understand the type of PFM reforms that have been implemented across the region in the last decade, including where these reforms have gone well, where they have not, and why. Beyond these questions, the study seeks to see if any broader conclusions can be drawn regarding the way in which these reforms have been implemented and how that has affected their success (or lack thereof). Are there tactical lessons about what works best during implementation from which future reformers can benefit? In what ways do broader political economy considerations shape and influence the challenge of PFM reform in MENA?

To review PFM reform across MENA, it is necessary to utilize a common approach to structure the analysis. In recent years, the Public Expenditure and Financial Accountability (PEFA) framework has become the most recognized and widely accepted tool for assessing the status of a given economy's PFM system. This set of 28 high-level indicators measures performance against best practice in developed and developing economies and allows progress to be tracked over time. The indicators analyze performance in the six core areas of public financial management spanning the budget process: (1) credibility of the budget; (2) comprehensiveness and transparency; (3) policy-based budgeting; (4) predictability and control in budget execution; (5) accounting, recording, and reporting; and (6) external audit. The central government is the main area of focus, along with issues relating to the overall scrutiny of public finances. Activities of public enterprises and subnational levels of government are not addressed directly.

While the PEFA indicators provide a point assessment of the PFM system for a particular economy, the focus of this study is on the reforms to the system and what progress is being made as a result of these reforms. To gain this insight, the PEFA analysis has been augmented by a series of economy chapters that are provided in Volume 2. These chapters were drafted along a common template to provide a more detailed picture of the PFM reform efforts in the economies of this study. These assessments have also sought to go beyond the "what" of PFM reform—where the analysis is organized around the six core PEFA areas—to capture some of the "how" and "why" of reform. This touches upon both strategies for implementation and broader political economy issues within a given economy. These chapters have relied heavily upon desk studies of existing Bank and Fund documents, such as Public Expenditure Reviews (PERs), Country Financial Accountability Assessments (CFAAs), Country Procurement Assessment Reports (CPARs), IMF Fiscal Reports on the Observance of Standards and Codes (ROSCs), as well as a variety of project-related documents.

In two cases of particularly interesting and far-reaching reform in MENA, the analysis relies on more detailed case studies. The first is Salam Fayyad's PFM reforms, which were implemented during his first tenure as Minister of Finance in the West Bank and Gaza from 2002 to 2005. The second are the reforms in tax and customs implemented in Egypt since 2005 under the tenure of Youssef Boutros Ghali. These reforms are singled out both because they were substantial in scope and are widely perceived to have made a material improvement to the existing systems.

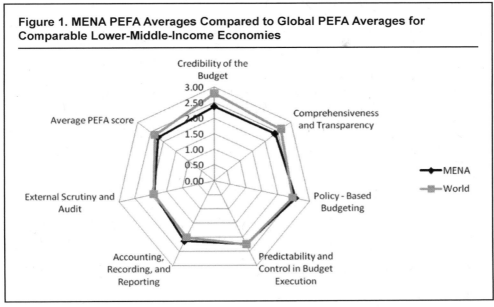

Figure 1. MENA PEFA Averages Compared to Global PEFA Averages for Comparable Lower-Middle-Income Economies

Source: World Bank.

MENA PFM Practices Compared Against Global Averages

Figure 1 provides the summary results for the six PEFA exercises that have been completed for economies in the study. Assessments for the West Bank and Gaza, and Syria were completed in 2006; Jordan in 2007; Iraq and the Republic of Yemen in 2008; and Morocco in 2009.[1] A PEFA analysis is currently underway in Tunisia, but has not been finalized. PEFA reviews have yet to be conducted for two other economies in this study: Algeria and Lebanon. The PEFA alpha scale has been converted to a numeric scale ranging from 0 to 4 to assist with comparisons, where 4 is the highest rating.

A comparative analysis was conducted as to where MENA economies stood vis-à-vis other economies at similar levels of development, in this case 19 lower-middle-income economies with GDPs from US$936 to US$3,075 per capita in 2007 who had recently completed a PFEA assessment. (Among the list of comparators were three economies from Africa; three from Latin America and the Caribbean; six from East Asia and the Pacific; and seven from Europe and Central Asia.[2]) The results are presented below.

At an aggregate level, MENA's PFM systems are roughly comparable to those of other economies at similar income levels. As a whole, the region tends to fare a bit better on accounting, recording, and reporting and a bit worse on credibility of the budget. Among the economies covered in this study, the highest ranked economies in aggregated PEFA rankings are Morocco and Jordan. They both have overall average scores of about B (2.87). On the lower end of the scale, the West Bank and Gaza and Iraq have PEFA assessments that would average around a C– (1.5 to 1.6), although the formal PEFA assessments do not include minus (–) rankings. In terms of average scores for the six main categories, the tightest scores (that is, the lowest standard deviation) were around credibility of the budget, indicating commonality among MENA economies on this dimension, whereas the largest average discrepancies were found in the area of budget comprehensiveness and transparency.

The Substantive Reform Agenda

This section is structured around 13 common categories of PFM reform grouped under six stages of the budget cycle. The selection of categories follows that used by Matt Andrews in an earlier study using PEFA data; however the categories have been adapted to reflect common reform activity in the MENA region.[3] Figure 2 sets out the different stages in the budget cycle and the reform categories considered at each stage

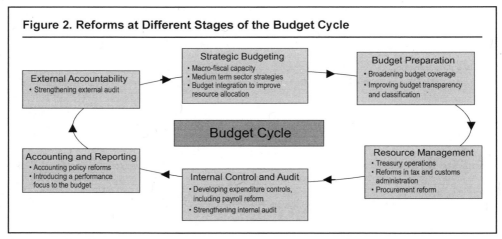

Figure 2. Reforms at Different Stages of the Budget Cycle

Source: World Bank.

The choice of reform categories involved a number of compromises, and several important reforms that have close links to PFM (for example, civil service reforms) are not considered. Determining whether to create separate categories for some wide-ranging reforms was also an issue. In particular, two common reforms—Medium Term Expenditure Framework (MTEF) and treasury reforms—often cover a number of the above categories. These reforms are considered in their component parts during the discussion. Conversely, reforms in budget transparency that occur at a variety of stages in the budget cycle (for example, budget documentation, in year financial reporting, and end of year financial statements) are considered in a single category.

For each of the six stages of the budget cycle, the relevant PEFA scores are first reported, followed by an assessment of each of the reform areas relevant to this stage. For each reform area, the report briefly sets out the underlying objective of this type of reform before reviewing experience in different MENA economies. It then provides an assessment of what has worked and what has proven to be more challenging.

1. Strategic Budgeting

Macro-fiscal Capacity and Budget Sustainability. Having a unit in the Ministry of Finance to provide macroeconomic and fiscal (macro-fiscal) policy advice is important for good aggregate fiscal management. The Ministries of Finance in the region have traditionally not had this capacity but, in recent years, a number of economies have established units to provide macro-fiscal advice. The work is analytically demanding and attracting suitable staff within standard civil service contracts has proven to be a challenge. In view of this, many of the units initially focused on monitoring taxes and preparing monthly reports on budget execution. However, as they have increased their capacity, they have become more involved in budget preparation through developing a fiscal framework for the budget—although the link between these frameworks and the final budget is still not strong.

Focusing on Medium Term Expenditures at the Sectoral Level. In fiscal management, the cost of a policy in the next year is not always a good indication of the costs over time. To better manage the budget, a number of economies in the MENA region are attempting to develop "forward estimates" of expenditures at the sectoral level as part of MTEF reforms. The reform is extremely resource intensive and, to date, the results have been disappointing. Often, the work has been carried out through pilot projects in various sectors with limited ownership from the Ministry of Finance. As a result, the estimates remain an analytical exercise which is not used in preparing the budget. Another weakness is that the analysis focuses only on project expenditures and insufficient attention is paid to recurrent expenditures, which generally form the bulk of the budget. While the argument for developing sector based forward estimates to provide a medium term perspective is compelling, this is a major reform and should only be initiated once more basic improvements to the PFM system have been completed.

Budget Integration to Improve Efficiency of Expenditure. All economies in the region continue to have elements of dual budgeting, with separate arrangements for deciding the allocations for operating and capital expenditures. These arrangements impede efforts to get the best value for money from expenditures, as they risk gaps or duplication of expenditure; inconsistent expenditures; and the wrong mix of expenditures both in aggregate and at the level of activities. While some progress has been made to integrate the presentation of the budget, efforts to integrate other elements of budget management have largely been elusive. In economies with a separate planning ministry managing the capital budget, institutional resistance to consolidating budget management in the Ministry of Finance has been a particular problem. Where consolidation of budget management within the Ministry of Finance does occur, one of the main challenges is to ensure that the Ministry has the necessary analytical capacity to oversee the capital budget. For this reason, the transition needs to be carefully planned.

2. Budget Preparation

Broadening Budget Scope and Coverage. Ensuring broad budget coverage is important to make the budget effective both as a tool for fiscal control and allocating resources to the highest priority area. It is also important to ensure that there is effective accountability for public expenditure. Limitations in the scope of the budget are a general problem in the region as reflected in low PEFA scores for unreported government expenditure. The technical demands of this reform are not significant and good progress has been made where there is sufficient political commitment. However, there are strong incentives for those with expenditures outside the budget to resist the change, and a strategic approach needs to be taken to the reform that anticipates the likely resistance from these interests.

Improving Budget Transparency and Classification. Better information on budgeted expenditures can play an important role in building the credibility of the government's fiscal policy with the public, parliament, and external financiers. Reforming the budget classification is an important component of this broader objective. Many economies in the region have taken steps to improve the transparency of the budget documents, update the budget classification, and introduce in-year budget reporting. These efforts have been among the most successful PFM reforms. One of the factors behind this success is that the reforms are seen as technical in nature and thus less susceptible to opposition from vested interests. The reforms also tend to rely on a small team of staff in the Ministry of Finance, which makes them better placed in an environment where the civil service has limited capacity. Moreover, once introduced the reforms have tended to become part of the fabric of the system and this has made them more enduring.

3. Resource Management

Developing Treasury Operations. A well functioning treasury system can minimize the government's net borrowing costs and reduce exposure to the risk of bank default. A number of the economies in the region have embarked on treasury reforms to improve cash management by establishing a treasury single account (TSA) at the central bank. While progress has been made, the coverage of the TSA is often not complete because the Ministry of Finance has not had the authority to consolidate some balances. A number of economies have set up units to prepare and maintain a cash plan, which can assist in aligning the borrowing and investment activity with the government's cash needs. However, too often the cash plans are not being actively used in cash management. Few economies have taken steps to improve debt management systems as part of treasury reforms.

Reforms in Revenue Administration: Tax and Customs. By improving the administration of the tax system, a government can increase the revenues it collects while enhancing the fairness of the system and reducing the cost of doing business for taxpayers. In general, MENA economies have made much better progress with tax administration reform than they have with expenditure management reforms. One reason for this is that Ministers of Finance have taken an active interest in the reforms as they are driven by a need to both increase revenues and improve the environment for doing business. Another factor is that tax administration is a distinct function within government and it has been possible to provide performance incentives to the staff of the tax authority that could not be applied generally across the public sector. One unhelpful consequence of this tactic has been that some of the better staff have moved to tax administration from expenditure roles within government, exacerbating existing capacity problems in these areas. For this reason, caution should be exercised in deciding whether to introduce incentives for tax administration in isolation.

Procurement Reform. The way in which the purchase of goods and services is controlled through the procurement process can help the government to minimize collusion and other corrupt practices. Improvements to the procurement procedures can therefore lower the cost of government expenditures. The procurement systems in the region are weak. Reforms have been attempted in a number of economies but the timescales for these reforms have been extended and the outcomes have been disappointing. The reforms often touch on areas of significant corruption and therefore can pose a threat to particular interests, which have strong incentives to delay or divert the process. The failure to make progress in large part reflects an unwillingness to confront these special interests.

4. Internal Control and Audit

Developing Expenditure Controls. Effective expenditure controls are important to support aggregate fiscal control, ensure that the allocation of resources reflected in the budget is followed, and that the government does not pay more than it needs to for goods and services. Because of the link to the transaction cycle, the controls are an important element in addressing corruption associated with government expenditure. The economies in the region tend to have extensive and time-consuming control systems (often evidenced by multiple approval signatures), but as evidenced in the PEFA assessments, these systems are not effective. Two key problems are that the overlaying controls diffuse accountability, and that they often only apply at the payment point rather than when expenditure is committed. Despite the problems being faced in the region, there have been relatively few attempts to streamline and strengthen the general control procedures. Progress has been made by some economies in payroll management, but this is uneven. The overall impression is that where there is a failure to make progress with improving expenditure controls, it is mainly due to a lack of genuine interest in the reforms from the authorities.

Strengthening Internal Audit. Internal audit aims at providing the executive with assurance of the quality of the financial management systems—in particular the implementation of financial controls and the management of risks.[4] Most economies in the region have weak internal audit functions reflecting problems in both the scope of audit activity, and conflicts of interest where the auditor is also part of the control function. Internal audit has in general not been given a high priority for reform in part because it is an advanced PFM reform. But resistance to change can also come from existing auditors who are reluctant to be removed from the transaction control process when this is a source of corruption.

5. Accounting and Reporting

Accounting Policy Reforms. Accounting reforms can improve the reliability with which expenditures and cash balances are controlled, monitored, and reported. Where accounting policies are aligned with international standards, there can be increased confidence in the integrity of the financial information presented. Experience with the reform of accounting systems in the region has been mixed. While most economies now operate double entry systems, there has been limited success in reforming accounting methodologies towards a consistent use of cash or accruals, as well as in applying international accounting standards. Because accounting reforms affect the work of many employees throughout the public sector, a strong commitment from the senior staff in the Ministry of Finance is essential if they are to be successfully introduced.

Introducing a Performance Focus to the Budget. The traditional input based budget does not provide policy makers with information on what goods, services, or policies are being financed by government expenditure. The idea of focusing on performance has been around for some time, and there is considerable interest in this reform from economies in the region. However, the successes to date are limited and the timeframe for the reform is proving to be extended. The reform is difficult in part because it relies on having many other elements of the PFM system operating at a reasonable standard.

For this reason, even where the reform proceeds, every effort should be made to avoid conceptually sophisticated approaches and to ensure that the approach can be supported by the accounting systems.

6. External Accountability

Strengthening External Audit. External audit provides parliament with assurance on the adherence to financial laws, the reliability of the financial statements, and value for money in government expenditure. As such, it provides an essential discipline on the financial management of the executive. The PEFA assessments indicate that the external audit functions of economies in the region have a range of weaknesses characterized by a strong focus on transactions rather than systems, as well as conflicts of interest where the auditor is part of the ex ante control system. In spite of the weaknesses in the audit bodies, there have been relatively few efforts to reform the external audit function, in part reflecting the relatively minor role played by parliaments in many economies in the region. While the focus of external audit is on providing assurance to parliament, the presence of an effective audit body can also support reforms in budget execution, by encouraging more discipline in the accounting practices. However, the success of efforts to build the capacity of the audit body will ultimately depend on whether the parliament is prepared to utilize the auditor's report.

Implementing Public Financial Management Reforms in MENA: An Emerging Set of Promising Practices?

Summarizing the discussion above, table 1 breaks MENA's experience with PFM reform down along three dimensions. The first category is reforms that have typically been more successful, in that a number of MENA economies have been able to implement them effectively and achieve concrete, independently verifiable improvements. The third category is comprised of reforms that have been historically been more challenging, difficult, and problematic. It does not mean that they have been impossible to implement, and some MENA economies may have been able to put in place certain elements of these reforms. But this is not common. The "mixed" category represents an area where generalizations across the region are difficult to make and the results are often more unique to a given economy.

The PFM reforms that have been particularly successful in MENA fall into two types: efforts to improve budget transparency and classification, and the reform of revenues, particularly tax and customs. Ironically, these represent two very different reforms. The

Table 1. Breakdown of Successful and Challenging PFM Reforms in MENA

Successful PFM Reforms	Mixed	Challenging PFM Reforms
• Improving budget classification • Improving budget transparency • Reforms in tax and customs	• Enhance macro-fiscal capacity • Budget integration • Streamlining ex ante control processes • Commitment control • Payroll management • Treasury operations • Reform of accounting systems • Internal and external audit	• Medium term sector strategies • Improving budget scope and coverage • Introducing performance into the budget • Procurement reforms • Large information technology projects

Source: World Bank.

first are relatively straightforward and technocratic in nature. An existing body of accepted practice exists to reform economic classification, such as in the form of the IMF's 2001 *Government Finance Statistics Manual* (GFSM), and there are incentives to align accounts along standard international practice to facilitate the production of comparable fiscal and economic data. While there may be some resistance to such reforms stemming from basic bureaucratic inertia, no fundamental interests are challenged or mandates threatened. Once implementation is complete, the reform becomes part of the fabric of the system and endures.

This is not true for reforms in tax and customs, where the stakes are much higher. Revenue agencies are often among the entities in government where problems of corruption are most pronounced, since their function places them in a position to extract rents from both firms and the general public. Efforts to restructure and reorganize such functions often encounter fierce resistance from both those on the inside and some on the outside. Yet if the challenges are great, the gains are often significant as well. For governments facing significant fiscal deficits, it is often more politically palatable to raise revenues—difficult as that may be—than to engage in painful cuts in expenditure. Such reforms are therefore able to garner the requisite high-level political support to see them through in spite of considerable opposition.

Unfortunately, on the other side of the spectrum are a host of reforms that are neither particularly easy to implement nor which bring the promise of substantial fiscal gains, at least in the short-term. Some, such as improving the scope and comprehensiveness of the budget, are not technically difficult to implement. However, as noted above, unless significant political capital is invested in overcoming bureaucratic resistance, these reforms are unlikely to move forward. Other reforms, such as the development of MTEFs and greater performance orientation into the budget, are often both technically demanding and run up against powerful vested interests. In many cases, their successful implementation may depend upon underlying systems, procedures, and practices being in place that may not exist. It is therefore not surprising that their implementation is frequently delayed or halted.

A variety of lessons have emerged from the individual case studies and the more detailed assessments of reforms in the West Bank and Gaza and Egypt. They are summarized in box 1 as the "Ten Principles of Implementation" for PFM reforms in MENA.

Box 1. Ten Principles of Implementation for PFM Reforms in MENA

1. Know the value—and limitations—of political economy analysis
2. PFM reform as means and not ends
3. Context matters, so swim with the current
4. The wisdom of "muddling through"— grand strategy versus incremental change
5. Establish basic systems before contemplating more advanced reforms
6. Whenever possible, keep reforms quick, simple and mutually reinforcing
7. Be wary of large financial management information systems
8. Internal challenges: leadership, coordination, skills and incentives
9. External stakeholders—useful, but don't count on them
10. Lessons for donors: be more strategic, selective, modest and flexible

Source: World Bank.

Lesson 1: Know the Value—and Limitations—of Political Economy Analysis. In many areas of governance and public administration reform including PFM, there has been a rush to embrace the discipline of political economy analysis (PEA) over the last decade. The field is still evolving and precise definitions are elusive, but at its core PEA analysis embodies the important observation that political and bureaucratic factors matter. Would be reformers should not mechanistically seek to transfer approaches and practices that work well in one setting to other very different institutional contexts.

Yet beyond this basic and sensible warning, the PEA literature has relatively little to contribute when it seeks to address the most important questions in any reform initiative: what should be done, when does it need to happen, who should do it and how. Each reform experience is unique and endogenous to a particular time and economy, as well as to an individual set of political, bureaucratic, institutional, and personal dynamics. PEA may be valuable in highlighting constraints or identifying potential supporters, and it can help to inform decisions about what is to be done. But the trajectories of the most successful reforms in MENA bear little resemblance to the type of recommendations that a typical donor-supported PEA would generate. PEA is not a substitute for solid strategic decision-making, and even less for astute tactical maneuvering during implementation. More is likely to be gained by investing in greater tactical flexibility, in terms of field-based governance advisors and public sector specialists who can provide real-time advice and assistance in high risk, high engagement settings, than in trying to perform more rigorous political and bureaucratic analysis up-front.

Lesson 2: PFM Reform as Means and Not Ends. PFM reforms arise from a number of different motives, ranging from the need to respond to an emergency to individual ministers seeking to make a career for themselves as reformers. In the MENA region, the most far-reaching reforms were implemented in response to an acute fiscal crisis and the need to fundamentally restructure tax practices to attract foreign investment. Under these circumstances, PFM reforms were effective in large part because they promised to be a solution—or at least part of the solution—to a broader set of problems. As such, senior political leaders were willing to push them through in the face of considerable resistance. Reforms that were implemented because they are consistent with emerging international best practice have typically lacked the staying power to overcome entrenched opposition.

Lesson 3: Context Matters, so Swim with the Current. A corollary of the observation that reforms are a means and not an end in themselves is the point that context matters. As noted above, two of the most far-reaching PFM reforms took place against a backdrop of an acute financial crisis, which gave them profile and visibility. However, major reform agendas can stretch over years, whereas the political and economic conditions that give rise to them are typically subject to much shorter time horizons. If reforms are largely technical in nature, have a solid rationale behind them are supported by well-positioned champions within the relevant ministries, and if they avoid alienating powerful constituencies, then under most circumstances they can probably stay "under the radar screen" and survive the shifting political, economic and administrative sands. Lebanon was able to implement some important reforms in payroll management, for example, even in the midst of a chronic political crisis and the absence of a functioning parliament.

But Lebanon's experience is also instructive, in that when these reforms have needed to move beyond the realm of what could be implemented by a Ministry of Finance decree and required broader cabinet or parliamentary approval, they have stalled. There are no examples of more far-reaching PFM reforms that came to fruition if the broader political context was not supportive. Nor are there examples of where senior officials were able to isolate and protect major PFM reforms from major shifts in the broader political climate. Put succinctly, an ebbing tide grounds all large boats—regardless of how well they are designed or the skill and determination of the captain.

Lesson 4: The Wisdom of "Muddling Through"—Grand Strategy versus Incremental Change. To what extent are MENA PFM reform agendas driven by an overarching strategic framework or integrated plan, versus a more flexible and improvised approach that seeks to take advantage of opportunities when they emerge? The answer is not entirely straightforward. On the one hand, MENA does not suffer from an absence of strategic plans for upgrading systems and procedures. Furthermore, there have been examples of when economies would have benefited from adopting a more comprehensive approach to PFM reform. The lack of a more comprehensive approach can be particularly problematic in the development of integrated financial management information systems, for example.

Yet while such reform strategies can be valuable as a statement of intent, communicating priorities, securing donor support or providing political cover for a given set of activities, their role in actually shaping successful reforms can be modest. The development of such plans is no guarantee that they will be implemented expeditiously. In many MENA economies, roll-out has taken much longer than expected, with a number of components being dropped or modified along the way. Nor are such plans a prerequisite for success. Salam Fayyad adopted a flexible view to West Bank and Gaza's PFM reforms, recognizing that he could not determine *a priori* the sequencing of reforms or expect to have control over the entire process. Fayyad describes his approach as being, "patient, deliberate, methodical, and opportunistic, looking for an opening here and there." His approach was informed by a clear set of priorities, but utilized tactical flexibility in terms of the sequencing and timing of reforms. Aspects of Egypt's tax reforms evolved in much the same way.

Lesson 5: Establish Basic Systems Before Contemplating More Advanced Reforms. The temptation is often irresistible for governments and international advisors to strive for quantum improvements in performance by adopting some cutting-edge practices from OECD economies in a developing economy context. More often than not, the result has been a litany of dashed expectations and failed reforms. In response, the Bank's *Public Expenditure Management Handbook* (1998) emphasizes the importance of "getting the basics" right before moving on to tackle more advance reforms.

The PFM reform experience within MENA largely bears this out. This has been particularly true with regard to two sets of initiatives that have been among the more technically advanced to be implemented to the region: the move to a MTEF and the effort to introduce greater performance orientation into the budget process. As noted above, both have shown themselves to be complicated and problematic to implement, in part because their realization has relied upon a number of preconditions to be in place before they can be effective, and in part because other senior officials have been generally unwilling to allow themselves to be bound by such initiatives.

Lesson 6: When Possible, Keep Reforms Quick, Simple, and Mutually Reinforcing. It is an accepted article of faith that major PFM reforms are difficult, complex undertakings that require years or sometimes decades to fully come to fruition. Laws and regulations must be drafted; longstanding practices restructured; political and administrative cultures changed; institutions built and capacities strengthened. To attempt such undertakings quickly, so the argument goes, is a recipe for poorly thought through implementation and eventual failure.

As with many managerial maxims, there is some truth to this contention. PFM reforms in a number of MENA economies, such as introducing MTEFs or greater performance orientation into the budget, do take a long time to implement. Yet there are also cases where reforms can be implemented quite quickly when the requisite political will exists. Reforms dedicated to expanding the scope and comprehensiveness and transparency of the budget, for example, can be implemented within weeks or months if the proper political will is in place. Furthermore, some of the more effective reforms were deliberately implemented with haste. Salam Fayyad wanted to generate confidence in the reform agenda by taking specific, quick steps that made an impression. He felt, rightly as it turned out, that reform would become more difficult with time. Otherwise, as has happened far too often in MENA, reform can become "business as usual" and lose any sense of priority or urgency.

A related question is whether to pilot reforms or roll them out whole. In MENA, pilot PFM reforms have been implemented in a wide variety of contexts. The answer to this question is highly contextual. On the positive side, pilots—particularly when combined with rigorous monitoring—provide an opportunity to gain valuable experience in identifying potential problems that could plague a set of PFM reforms and rectifying them before too much damage is done. This is particularly important when the roll-out is likely to be time-consuming and expensive, as is the case with large IT systems. However, in the absence of firm commitment to proceed with a given set of reforms, pilots can often become an excuse for delay and inaction. Sometimes it is preferable to roll out reforms broadly and accept that there will be challenges during the early stages of implementation. Pilots also tend to do better in administrations with a history of experimentation and innovation than those with fixed traditions embedded in a strong legal framework.

Lesson 7: Be Wary of Large Financial Management Information Systems. An integrated financial management information system (IFMIS) can offer great benefits for a variety of PFM activities, especially budget execution. All economies in the region have made some effort to introduce computerized systems to support PFM. In general, two different strategies have been adopted: (1) develop a "sophisticated" fully integrated IFMIS; or (2) use a simple customized IT system to support budget execution. While there are some small successes to date, most of the "sophisticated" projects have struggled to meet their implementation milestones, budgets and promised functionality. When things go wrong, such IT failures can be extraordinarily costly, as was illustrated with the recent failure of a US$30 million FMIS system in Iraq. A number of problems have undermined these large projects, but two important concerns are weak project management arrangements and inadequate commitment and/or engagement of staff of the Ministry of Finance to the reform. Would-be reformers looking to import sophisticated IT solutions should proceed with caution in both MENA and elsewhere.

The second approach has been to develop simple computerized systems with limited functionality to help support budget execution. The systems are usually customized to fit the specific needs of the budget execution system of the economy. They tend to have much lower initial development costs, and provided their objectives remain minimal, they may also be an efficient way of exposing officials only familiar with paper based operations to the potential of a future IFMIS. However, there are limitations to this approach. First, because the systems are developed to order, they often do not include standard functionality that has proven useful in other systems. Second, the systems tend to be less flexible in dealing with new user requirements than off the shelf systems. While the initial cost of the system may not be high, these costs increase over time as the system is reconfigured for new developments. For these reasons, the use of a simple system should be seen as a short term solution with the eventual aim of moving to an integrated system.

Lesson 8: Internal Challenges: Leadership, Coordination, and Incentives. MENA's reform experience holds a number of important lessons as to how such reforms should be structured and organized. The most far reaching and successful reforms within MENA have been driven by powerful ministers of finance, whose role is pivotal in the process. Both Salam Fayyad in the West Bank and Gaza and Youssef Boutros Ghali in Egypt brought a combination of impressive technical expertise and a solid technical of the issues, along with considerable political and managerial savvy and sheer determination.

There is a wide array of stakeholders in any PFM reform initiative, including ministries, agencies, departments, subnational entities, and state owned enterprises. The quality of coordination between these agencies and the MOF varies both within and between economies, but it is frequently problematic and occasionally dysfunctional. To cope with such problems, several economies have established inter-agency task forces and other mechanisms to facilitate coordination. Their structure and membership can vary without unduly compromising their prospects for success. More problematic is the fact that, while such coordinating bodies can be relatively easy to establish, in a number of cases they end up meeting only infrequently thus compromising the quality of implementation.

MENA economies have adopted a variety of approaches to gain access to the requisite expertise. Some have relied heavily upon project implementation units staffed largely by external experts, whereas others have sought to keep these reforms in-house. While each approach has its strengths and weaknesses, some general lessons have emerged. The first is that technically skilled and managerially adept leadership is required at the project management level—and such leaders need to be fully empowered—or the reforms are unlikely to succeed. Second, capacity constraints at the team level are often not taken seriously enough in designing reforms. Efforts to work around a lack of capacity by relying too heavily upon external experts or local staff recruited specifically for the task are a Faustian bargain; they need to be carefully planned and managed with a clear exit strategy in mind. Finally, MENA governments have often chronically underinvested in the careful monitoring of reforms.

Lesson 9: External Stakeholders—Useful, but Don't Count on Them. As a general rule, the Executive Branch is extremely powerful throughout MENA. Other stakeholders—be they legislative or judicial branches, various civil society organizations, academics, think tanks, or the private sector—operate at a distinct disadvantage when it comes to influencing political and administrative decision-making. This is particularly true with regard to PFM reform, which is often viewed as a narrow, specialized, and technocratic field.

Throughout the region, parliaments have been growing in influence but still typically lack the staff and committee structures that would allow them to provide detailed

CHAPTER 1

Introduction: Public Financial Management Reform in MENA and Beyond

In the early stages of the state, taxes are light in their incidence, but fetch in a large revenue...As time passes and kings succeed each other, they lose their tribal habits in favor of more civilized ones. Their needs and exigencies grow ... owing to the luxury in which they have been brought up. Hence they impose fresh taxes on their subjects ... sharply raise the rate of old taxes to increase their yield.... But the effects on business of this rise in taxation make themselves felt. For business men are soon discouraged by the comparison of their profits with the burden of their taxes.... Consequently production falls off, and with it the yield of taxation.

Ibn Khaldun (1332–1406)

The Importance of Public Financial Management

One of the most important functions that governments perform is mobilizing financial resources and deploying them to achieve their objectives. According to the most recent World Bank data, governments throughout the Middle East and North Africa (MENA) region spent approximately US$407 billion dollars in 2007 in delivering their policy, regulatory and service functions. The way in which this money is spent has huge implications for their broader development trajectory. For example, a one percent efficiency gain in the Arab Republic of Egypt's budget for 2009 would yield US$637 million dollars—enough resources to build 40,000 schools, pave 4,500 kilometers of highway, or recruit an additional 600,000 doctors. It is therefore not surprising that issues of public financial management, or PFM, have been at the heart of governance reform programs in virtually all of the economies in the region.

In the BBC parody of government life, *Yes Minister*, the consummate British bureaucrat, Sir Humphrey Appleby, once wryly observed: "the Treasury does not work out what it needs and then thinks how to raise the money. It pitches for as much as it can get away with and then thinks how to spend it." While such thinking has not been entirely banished from public sectors around the globe, the PFM agenda has moved quite a bit since this episode first aired in January 1986. Over the past two decades, there has been relentless pressure in both developed and developing economies to improve the quality of public expenditure and generate more value for money from government operations.

For governments to perform their spending function well, their PFM practices should meet certain well-established criteria. Government spending should be affordable, in that it takes place within a macroeconomic framework which ensures that the level of spending is consistent with the government's monetary and fiscal policy objectives and is sustainable in the long term. Governments should optimize the allocation of public resources between different sectors and expenditure categories in a way that reflects their policy priorities, including sustainable growth as well as human and social development. Such expenditure should be efficient, in that it maximizes output for a given set of inputs, and effective, in that it supports the successful realization of the government's goals. It should also be transparent; conducted in accordance with the relevant laws and regulations; and undertaken with appropriate checks and balances to ensure financial probity.

In many MENA economies, PFM reforms have been on the agenda for a decade or more. Some are seeking to implement basic financial management and information systems that will ensure resources are spent in a timely fashion for the purposes intended. Others are pursuing changes that will allow for greater efficiency and predictability in spending, along with an enhanced focus on performance and value for money. Many are dealing with issues such as enhancing transparency, ensuring adequate internal and external audit, or expanding the scope and comprehensiveness of the budget.

This report seeks to reflect upon this experience and better understand the nature of the PFM challenges confronting the economies of the MENA region. Turning to the substance of these reforms, it asks where are they performing well and where are they struggling? To what extent are these economies dealing with common problems stemming from similar administrative traditions and comparable levels of development, or unique challenges grounded within their own particular historical or bureaucratic experience? The analysis also seeks to understand the type of PFM reforms that have been implemented across the region in the last decade, including where these reforms have gone well, where they have not, and why.

Beyond these questions, the study seeks to see if any broader conclusions can be drawn regarding the way in which these reforms have been implemented and how that has affected their success (or lack thereof). How do broader political economy considerations shape and influence the challenge of PFM reform in MENA? Are there tactical lessons about what works best during implementation from which future reformers can benefit?

This report is divided into two volumes. The first volume summarizes the results and presents the conclusions of this analysis. The second provides the individual economy case studies and templates upon which many of these conclusions are based.

Beyond MENA: The Lessons from Global Experience

The MENA PFM reforms have not taken place in a vacuum. Throughout the globe, a variety of reforms have been implemented over the past two to three decades under the general rubric of "New Public Management." The scope and content of these reforms has varied, but they have generally included providing greater responsibility and control over inputs to managers in exchange for greater accountability for outputs; moving to a multiyear framework in budget execution linked to realistic fiscal policy and revenue estimates; shifting from cash accounting to accrual accounting; and moving from compliance auditing to performance auditing, among others. Many of these reforms were introduced in OECD economies and then migrated to MENA and other developing economies in varying degrees—or at least attempts were made to transpose them. Against these trends, an opposing "getting the basics right" school emerged that emphasized the need for essential systems to be in place and functioning well before moving on to advanced reforms. PFM reforms in MENA and elsewhere have tended to reflect elements of both approaches—the desire to adopt more "cutting edge" practices across a range of fields and sub-fields, such as introducing more performance orientation, Medium Term Expenditure Frameworks (MTEFs), and financial management information systems, as well as the need to ensure that the essential prerequisites are in place first.

Issues of public finance reform have been at the core of the World Bank's work on governance for over two decades. A recent survey of support for public sector reform by the Bank's Independent Evaluation Group (IEG) reviewed the Bank's work on PFM issues throughout the globe.[1] The report noted that between 1990 and 2006 the Bank approved 467 lending projects with significant public sector reform components. Of these, public financial management was by far the most common theme, comprising 81 percent of the public sector projects approved during this period. PFM work was also heavily represented in Bank analytical and advisory activities and institutional development grants. Furthermore, the Bank's work on PFM issues has increased sharply since the 1990s.

The IEG report concluded that the Bank's increased PFM lending and analytical work can be linked with encouraging PFM improvements among borrowers, usefully adapting PFM tools from other jurisdictions, and carrying out effective monitoring with robust assessment tools, such as PEFA.[2] However, progress has been uneven. The report argued that Bank performance might have achieved greater success with deeper institutional and governance analysis, greater attention to addressing basic systems before moving to advanced PFM tools and techniques, and more Bank support and flexibility in working to improve economy procurement systems. It also noted that some specific reforms, such as moving to a MTEF, have been successful in some contexts but challenging in many others.

Other assessments have sounded similar themes, arguing for both a widening and a deepening of reforms to engage a broader set of stakeholders while simultaneously underscoring the need for more attention to domestic politics and established practices and institutions.[3] They have argued that PFM reform is a long-term endeavor, in which failure is often attributed more to implementation than the technical aspects of the program. Reforms such as MTEFs and expenditure controls have tended to move forward slowly, as have those involving large computerized information systems and the reform of audit institutions.

This analysis will argue that in a number of important areas, such findings are consistent with the experience of PFM reform in MENA. In particular, MENA economies have struggled to implement many of the PFM reforms that have been problematic elsewhere. Yet there are also important points of divergence, particularly with regard to the prescriptions for implementation. It may be that MENA poses some unique challenges that are not present elsewhere. Or it may be that our understanding of how such reforms are actually implemented in many economies around the globe needs to be further refined.

What Is "MENA"? Selecting the Economies for This Study

At a broader level, the question of how to define the Middle East and North Africa region is a thorny one that raises a host of complex and occasionally contentious issues. The definition utilized in this analysis is a strictly bureaucratic one. The World Bank's MENA region consists of 19 economies, stretching from Morocco in the west to Oman and the Islamic Republic of Iran in the east. It includes Djibouti but not Mauritania or Sudan. As of 2007 (the most recent year for which statistics are available), average GNI per capita across the region is around US$2,795, a figure that places it roughly in the company of East Asia and the Pacific (US$2,190). It is well below Europe and Central Asia (US$6,013) and Latin America and the Caribbean (US$5,888), but ahead of South Asia (US$879) and Sub-Saharan Africa (US$966).

This study surveys PFM reforms across a range of 10 economies in the MENA region: Algeria, the Arab Republic of Egypt, Iraq, Jordan, Lebanon, Morocco, Syria, Tunisia, the West Bank and Gaza and the Republic of Yemen. They were selected partly because they represent economies where the Bank has been heavily engaged on PFM issues and been able to gather a wealth of comparative information (although Syria is an example of an economy where a diagnostic has been performed but the engagement has been more limited). They also represent an interesting cross-section of administrative traditions and different levels of development. Table 1.1 captures a number of characteristics for each economy, ranging from GDP per capita to literacy and life expectancy rates to internet penetration. At the high end, Lebanon has a GDP per capita of US$6,017 and a life expectancy of 72 years, whereas at the other end of the spectrum, these figures stand at US$973 and 62 years for the Republic of Yemen. Jordan has around 38.3 internet users per 100 citizens, as opposed to only .9 for Iraq. Taken together, these economies are home to over 70 percent of MENA's population and just under a third of its GDP. Many of the findings from this analysis will be of relevance to other MENA economies as well.

Table 1.1. Basic Statistics on MENA Economies Selected for PFM Analysis

	Economy	Population	GDP (US$ mil)	GDP per capita	Life expectancy at birth	Literacy	Internet use per capita
1	Algeria	33,858,168	136,034	4,018	72	70	10
2	Egypt, Arab Rep.	80,060,540	130,473	1,630	70	71	15
3	Iraq	29,947,491	62,000	2,070	68	74	1
4	Jordan	5,718,855	17,005	2,974	72	90	21
5	Lebanon	4,162,450	25,047	6,017	72	87	38.3
6	Morocco	31,224,136	75,226	2,373	71	52	21
7	Syrian Arab Republic	20,082,697	40,549	2,019	74	80	17
8	Tunisia	10,225,400	35,020	3,425	74	74	17
9	West Bank and Gaza	3,832,185	4,016	1,048	73	92	9
10	Yemen, Rep.	22,269,306	21,658	973	62	59	1
	Total	**241,381,228**	**547,029**				
	% of MENA	**67.9%**	**31.5%**				

Source: World DataBank: http://databank.worldbank.org/ddp/home.do?Step=3&id=4Source: All data is for 2007 or most recent year available.

To differing degrees, the largest group of economies shares a French colonial heritage, including Morocco, Algeria, Tunisia, Lebanon, and Syria. The French colonial administration left behind a functioning bureaucracy and well-defined legal framework. In these economies, as in many other civil code jurisdictions, the law plays a prominent role in many facets of public administration, including PFM. Egypt, Jordan, West Bank and Gaza, Iraq and, to a lesser extent, the Republic of Yemen experienced varying degrees of British colonization. This was more deeply rooted in the former People's Democratic Republic of Yemen (also known as South Yemen), where Aden was colonized from 1839 to 1967, and in Egypt, which was colonized from 1882 to 1923. As with French colonization, the most lasting legacy has tended to be the civil administration and the legal background. As late as the fall of Saddam Hussein in Iraq, for example, the budget director in the Ministry of Finance relied on manuals and regulations dating from the British era.

While these economies come from disparate legal and administrative backgrounds, they share a number of features in common. Their Arabic language and Islamic heritage support a shared sense of identity. Most achieved independence around the same time, and in a number of cases their constitutions and legal frameworks were derived from similar sources. Their public sectors tend to be large and expensive, reflecting the need to absorb excess employment, as well as the statist or dirigiste principles that encapsulated the prevailing wisdom during their political formation in the 1940s and 1950s. Political movements such as pan-Arabism, and political parties, such as the Ba'ath, often had cross-border connections, as did many of the royal families through ties of blood and marriage. All of these factors have reinforced a sense of collective identity.

Beyond these cultural and historical linkages, there are numerous integrative institutions that reinforce this sense of collective character within the MENA region. The most prominent is the Arab League, or to give it its correct title, the League of Arab States, which has 22 members. While the Arab League typically deals with broader political issues, it has on occasion addressed the "good governance" agenda as well through forums such as the Alexandria Declaration in May 2004. While focusing mostly on legal and political reforms, the declaration also contained references to minimizing bureaucracy and increasing government efficiency, as well as encouraging privatization programs and passing laws that would obligate authorities to produce economic data and make it available and easily accessible. Of more specific interest to PFM reform agenda are groups such as the Arab Organization of Supreme Audit Institutions (ARABOSAI), a regional group of the International Organization of Supreme Audit Institutions (INTOSAI) with 21 members.[4] The UNDP and OECD's MENA Initiative on Governance and Investment for Development has recently began establishing a network of senior budget officials patterned after similar networks in Central and Eastern Europe. These organizations promote good practice among members and hold regular meetings to discuss issues of mutual interest.

Using the PEFA Ranking to Evaluate PFM in MENA

To review PFM reform across MENA, it is necessary to utilize a common framework of analysis. In recent years, the Public Expenditure and Financial Accountability (PEFA) framework has become the most recognized and widely accepted tool for assessing the status of a given economy's PFM system. This set of 28 high-level indicators measures performance against best practice in developed and developing economies and allows progress to be tracked over time. An additional three indicators are used to track donor practices in heavily aid dependent settings.

The indicators analyze performance in the six core areas of public financial management spanning the budget process: (1) credibility of the budget; (2) comprehensiveness and transparency; (3) policy-based budgeting; (4) predictability and control in budget execution; (5) accounting, recording, and reporting; and (6) external audit. The central government is the main area of focus, along with issues relating to the overall scrutiny of public finances. Activities of public enterprises and subnational levels of government are not addressed directly.

PEFA was not initially developed to facilitate cross economy comparisons, but it is increasingly being used for this purpose. Paolo de Renzio, for example, recently compared the results of 57 PEFA assessments conducted prior to August 2007, including three from the MENA region (Jordan, Syria and the West Bank and Gaza).[5] Although at that point, the MENA sample was too small to draw any robust conclusions, de Renzio highlighted several interesting findings, including the large variation between average scores, the tendency for rankings to fall off as one progresses from budget formulation through implementation to audit and accountability, and the utility in focusing on more narrow comparisons across certain sub-sets of economies.

Table 1.2 provides the summary results for the six PEFA assessments that have been completed for economies in the study. Assessments for the West Bank and Gaza and Syria were completed in 2006; Jordan in 2007; Iraq and the Republic of Yemen in 2008; and Morocco in 2009.[6] A PEFA analysis is currently underway in Tunisia, but has not been finalized. It has yet to be conducted for two other economies in this study: Algeria and Lebanon.

The PEFA alpha scale has been converted to a numeric scale ranging from 0 to 4 to assist with comparisons, where 4 is the highest rating. It should be noted that, while all PEFA assessments use the same framework, the scores reflect the judgment of the assessment team. Therefore undue weight should not be given to small differences across economies. Furthermore, PEFA is a tool that is applied to all economies—both developed and developing—which may also have an impact upon the MENA rankings.

A comparative analysis was conducted as to where MENA economies stood vis-à-vis other economies at similar levels of development, in this case 19 lower-middle-income economies with GDPs from US$936 to US$3,075 per capita in 2007 who had recently completed PFEA assessment. (Among the list of comparators were three economies from Africa; three from Latin America and the Caribbean; six from East Asia and the Pacific; and seven from Europe and Central Asia.)[7] The results are presented in figure 1.1.

At an aggregate level, MENA's PFM systems are roughly comparable to those of other economies at similar income levels. As a whole, the region tends to do a bit better on accounting, recording and reporting, and a bit worse on credibility of the budget. (See the Appendix for a more detailed breakdown.)

Among the economies covered in this study, the highest ranked economies in aggregated PEFA rankings are Morocco and Jordan. They both have overall average scores of about B (2.87). On the lower end of the scale, West Bank and Gaza (West Bank and Gaza) and Iraq have PEFA Assessments that would average around a C– (1.5 to 1.6), although

Table 1.2. PEFA Scores for the MENA Economies in the Study

		Algeria	Egypt, Arab Rep.	Iraq	Jordan	Lebanon	Morocco	Syrian Arab Republic	Tunisia	West Bank & Gaza	Yemen, Rep.	Average Score
Credibility of the Budget	Aggregate expenditure out-turn compared to original approved budget	NA	NA	1.00	4.00	NA	4.00	2.00	NA	3.00	1.00	2.50
	Composition of expenditure out-turn compared to original approved budget	NA	NA	2.00	1.00	NA	2.00	1.00	NA	2.00	2.00	1.67
	Aggregate revenue out-turn compared to original approved budget	NA	NA	4.00	4.00	NA	4.00	3.00	NA	3.00	4.00	3.67
	Stock and monitoring of expenditure payment arrears	NA	NA	1.00	1.00	NA	2.33	NA	NA	1.33	-	1.42
	Average score for Credibility of the Budget			2.00	2.50		3.08	2.00		2.33	2.33	2.37
Comprehensiveness and Transparency	Classification of the budget	NA	NA	2.00	4.00	NA	4.00	1.00	NA	1.00	2.00	2.33
	Comprehensiveness of information included in budget documentation	NA	NA	1.00	4.00	NA	3.00	1.00	NA	3.00	4.00	2.67
	Extent of unreported government operations	NA	NA	1.33	3.00	NA	2.33	2.00	NA	2.33	3.33	2.39
	Transparency of Inter-Governmental Fiscal Relations	NA	NA	1.00	3.33	NA	2.00	2.33	NA	1.33	4.00	2.33
	Oversight of aggregate fiscal risk from other public sector entities	NA	NA	1.00	3.33	NA	3.00	2.00	NA	1.33	2.00	2.11
	Public Access to key fiscal information	NA	NA	1.00	3.00	NA	4.00	1.00	NA	2.00	2.00	2.17
	Average score for Comprehensiveness and Transparency			1.22	3.44		3.06	1.56		1.83	2.89	2.33
Policy-Based Budgeting	Orderliness and participation in the annual budget process	NA	NA	2.00	3.33	NA	4.00	3.33	NA	2.33	4.00	3.17
	Multi-year perspective in fiscal planning, expenditure policy and budgeting	NA	NA	1.33	3.33	NA	2.33	1.33	NA	1.00	3.00	2.05
	Average score for Policy - Based Budgeting			1.67	3.33		3.17	2.33		1.67	3.50	2.61
Predictability and Control in Budget Execution	Transparency of taxpayer obligations and liabilities	NA	NA	3.00	3.00	NA	4.00	NA	NA	NA	3.00	3.25
	Effectiveness of measures for taxpayer registration and tax assessment	NA	NA	2.00	2.33	NA	3.33	NA	NA	NA	3.00	2.67
	Effectiveness in collection of tax payments	NA	NA	1.33	3.00	NA	3.33	NA	NA	NA	1.33	2.25
	Predictability in the availability of funds for commitment of expenditures	NA	NA	2.33	4.00	NA	2.33	1.33	NA	1.33	1.33	2.11
	Recording and management of cash balances, debt and guarantees	NA	NA	2.00	3.33	NA	4.00	2.33	NA	2.00	3.33	2.83
	Effectiveness of payroll controls	NA	NA	1.33	3.00	NA	3.33	1.33	NA	2.33	1.33	2.11
	Competition, value for money and controls in procurement	NA	NA	1.33	3.00	NA	3.00	1.00	NA	NA	1.33	1.93
	Effectiveness of internal controls for non-salary expenditure	NA	NA	1.33	3.00	NA	2.33	3.33	NA	1.33	1.33	2.11
	Effectiveness of internal audit	NA	NA	1.33	2.00	NA	2.33	2.33	NA	2.00	1.33	1.89
	Average score for Predictability and Control in Budget Execution			1.78	2.96		3.11	1.94		1.80	1.92	2.25

Source: World Bank.

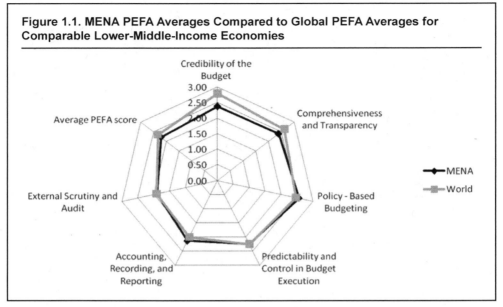

Figure 1.1. MENA PEFA Averages Compared to Global PEFA Averages for Comparable Lower-Middle-Income Economies

Source: World Bank.

the formal PEFA assessments do not include minus (−) rankings. In terms of average scores for the six main categories, the tightest scores (that is, the lowest standard deviation) were around credibility of the budget, indicating commonality among MENA economies on this dimension, whereas the largest average discrepancies were found in the area of budget comprehensiveness and transparency.

It is also interesting to note that there is a fairly high correlation between PEFA scores along various dimensions and the World Bank Institute's World Governance Indicators for controlling corruption in MENA (which, in turn, are tightly correlated with Transparency International's corruption rankings). The R^2 value is around .92 and the correlation coefficient is .86, indicating that states that do well on PEFA also tend to do well on controlling corruption. However, given the small sample size, it is more difficult to make judgments about causality even though the R^2 values and correlation coefficients are relatively high.

Though there is a large range in the overall economy averages for the PEFA assessment, it is clear that the region as a whole has progressed in some areas more than others. This is best assessed at the level of subcategory because of the variability of scores within each category.

Where MENA Has Ranked Consistently Higher

When reviewing the MENA region's individual PEFA scores, four dimensions stand out as areas of strength. They include aggregate revenue outturns compared to the original approved budget; the comprehensives of information included in budget document; the orderliness and participation in the budget process; and the transparency of taxpayer obligations and liabilities. Each is discussed in greater detail below.

Aggregate Revenue Outturn Compared to Original Approved Budget. Most economies scored solid A's (4.0) in this subcategory, which is part of the section "Credibility of the Budget." The exceptions were West Bank and Gaza and Syria, which both scored a B (3.0). This indicates that the economies were meeting, or exceeding, the forecast future revenue flows and therefore could be confident about financing the budget. Over-achieving the revenue projection often occurs where conservative assumptions are used—particularly when projecting petroleum revenues. While the PEFA system does not penalize economies that exceed the revenue projections included in the budget, it should be noted that this outcome can lead to a problems where the "excess" revenue is distributed as part of a supplementary budget during the year. This is the subcategory with the lowest standard deviation among all 28 indicators, indicating the tightest clustering among economies.

Comprehensiveness of Information Included in Budget Documentation. This subcategory falls within the section, "Comprehensiveness and Transparency." A number of economies scored A's (4.0) in this subcategory, but the average was reduced by very low scores for Syria and Iraq, which both scored a D (1.0). The scores suggest that the economies who have taken an interest in the issue have made good progress.

Orderliness and Participation in the Budget Process. Most economies scored well in this subcategory, which is in the section "Policy Based Budgeting." The Republic of Yemen and Morocco stood out with A's (4.0), while the main exception was Iraq with a C (2.0). This indicates that budgets are generally prepared on time and follow a well defined process—although it makes no comment about the quality of the budget that is prepared.

Transparency of Taxpayer Obligations and Liabilities. This subcategory, which is in the section "Predictability and Control of Budget Execution," was an area in which the region did particularly well (scores of A's and B's for all economies).

Where MENA Has Ranked Consistently Lower

There are a number of elements of the PEFA where the scores are consistently weak. They include the composition of expenditure outturns compared to the original approved budget; the effectiveness of internal audit; the quality and timeliness of annual financial statements; and external scrutiny and audit.

Composition of Expenditure Outturns Compared to Original Approved Budget. This subcategory is in the section "Credibility of the Budget" and received poor rankings. All economies scored a C (2.0), with the exception of Syria and Jordan which both scored D's (1.0). The low scores could reflect a number of problems. Either there are weaknesses in the budget that result in inappropriate allocations, or there are inadequate controls exerted during budget execution. This was the subcategory with the highest standard deviation, indicating the greatest discrepancy between economies.

Effectiveness of Internal Audit. This subcategory is within the section, "Predictability and Control in Budget Execution," and was consistently low throughout the region. The MENA economies scored between a C+ (2.33) and D (1.0). The subcategory, "Competition, Value for Money and Controls in Procurement," is another area requiring improvement, with low scores for all economies other than Morocco and Jordan, which had B's (3.0).

Quality and Timeliness of Annual Financial Statements. This subcategory is part of the section, "Accounting, Recording, and Reporting," and had modest rankings throughout the region (between C+ and D+, or 2.33 and 1.33). The low score could reflect poor quality accounting systems, or the low importance attached to the external audit function.

External Scrutiny and Audit. This category of the PEFA assessment had the lowest average scores. The subcategories, "Scope, Nature and Follow-up of External Audit" and "Legislative Scrutiny of External Audit Reports" ranked low in every MENA economy, ranging from a score of C+ to D. The exception was the Republic of Yemen, which scored a B+ in "Scope, Nature, and Follow-up of External Audit." This reflects weaknesses in both the capacity of the external audit body and of the legislative body charged with follow up on the reports that are prepared, as well as the general preeminence of the executive vis-à-vis the legislative branches

MENA Economy Templates and Case Studies on PFM Reform

While the PEFA data provides an important overview, it tells only part of the story. Future PEFA exercises will allow for benchmarking progress, but the exercise is relatively new in the region and currently they provide a one-time snapshot of the quality of PFM practices within a given economy. To gain a more comprehensive and dynamic picture, this analysis has been augmented by a series of economy chapters, which are provided in Volume 2. These chapters were drafted along a common template and have sought to utilize a modified PEFA framework to provide a more nuanced picture of the PFM reform efforts in the economies of this study. These assessments have also sought to go beyond the "what" of PFM reform and capture some of the "how" and "why" behind the reforms, touching upon both strategies for implementation and broader political economy issues within a given economy.

In two cases of particularly interesting and far-reaching reform in MENA, the analysis relies on more detailed case studies. The first is Salam Fayyad's PFM reforms, which were implemented during his first tenure as Minister of Finance in West Bank and Gaza from 2002 to 2005. The second are the reforms in tax policy and administration that have been implemented in Egypt since 2004 under the tenure of Youssef Boutros Ghali.[8] These reforms are singled out both because they were substantial in scope and are widely perceived to be the most successful of their type within the MENA region. They are the subject of more detailed World Bank case studies being developed through a joint case writing program between the Bank and the Dubai School of Government.[9]

Finally, it is worth stating that the PEFA scores do not in themselves provide a guide to the relative priority that should be given to reform activity. They are an important indicator but the assessment of priorities requires a fuller analysis. For example, if an economy has sizable expenditure arrears then it may be more important to raise a score from 2 to 3 in this indicator than to improve a score of 1 in another area. Similarly, a low score on the transparency of inter-government relations will have different implications for an economy with a highly decentralized system from one that is dominated by the central government.

Notes

1. World Bank, *Public Sector Reform: What Works and Why?* 2008.

2. Ibid, p. 51.

3. Carole and Nico Pretorius, *Public Financial Management Reform Literature*, United Kingdom Department for International Development Evaluation Working Paper, 2009.

4. See http://www.arabosai.org/en/index.asp.

5. Paolo de Renzio, *What do PEFA Assessments tell us about PFM Reforms across Countries?* Overseas Development Institute Working Paper No. 302, 2009.

6. Although a PEFA was presented for Egypt in October 2009, it remains preliminary, as the government has not endorsed a number of the findings.

7.   The economies incorporated into this analysis include the Republic of Congo, Lesotho, Swaziland, the Dominican Republic, Paraguay, Peru, Indonesia, Samoa, Timor-Leste, Tonga, Tuvalu, Vanuatu, Albania, Armenia, Azerbaijan, Kosovo, the former Yugoslav Republic of Macedonia, Moldova, and Ukraine.

8. The analysis of Salam Fayyad's reforms is captured in Nithya Nagarajan, *Reforms in Public Financial Management: West Bank and Gaza*, and Nithya Nagarajan, *Egypt: Overhaul of Tax Policy and Administration* (World Bank and Dubai School of Government: MENA Governance Case Program, 2010). Egypt's reforms in tax administration are captured in a *Doing Business* case study by Rita Ramalho, *Adding a Million Taxpayers* (World Bank: Doing Business, 2008).

9. Since 2005, the World Bank has been working with the Dubai School of Government to identify and draft cases on indigenous examples of governance and public sector reform drawn from throughout the MENA region. These cases will be published in a book, *Public Management Reform in the Middle East and North Africa: The Lessons of Experience for a Region in Transition*, which will be published by the World Bank in 2012.

CHAPTER 2

The Substance of Public Financial Management Reform: What Reforms Are Needed and Which Are Working?

In warfare everything is simple.
But the simple is often quite difficult.

Karl von Clauswitz

Although Clauswitz's famous dictum focuses on a more elemental field of human endeavour, it could easily apply to the discipline of public financial management (PFM). At one level, the goals of PFM are obvious and straightforward. Spend money efficiently within an envelope that is affordable and sustainable, in accordance with established procedures, on activities that will maximize an economy's long-term development potential. But while the objectives are simple, their realization is typically anything but.

This section reviews the main PFM reforms being pursued by economies in the region. The aim is to highlight which reforms are making progress (and which are not), as well as to set out some of the technical issues associated with the reforms. The analysis draws from the economy case studies in Volume 2 and is structured around some common categories of PFM reform. The selection of categories follows the work of Andrews, who assesses reforms at six different stages of the budget cycle. However the categories have been adapted to reflect common reform activity in the MENA region. Figure 2.1 sets out the different stages in the budget cycle and the reform categories considered at each stage.

The choice of reform categories involved a number of compromises and several important reforms that have close links to PFM are not considered. For example, tax and expenditure policy reforms, and civil service reforms are often closely associated with the reform of the PFM system. However, these reform areas are not included in the PEFA framework and including them in the study would have extended the analysis.

Determining whether to create separate categories for some wide-ranging reforms was also an issue. In particular, two common reforms—Medium Term Expenditure Frameworks (MTEFs) and treasury reforms—often cover a number of the above categories. These reforms are considered in their component parts during the discussion. In particular, components of MTEF are considered under both macro fiscal capacity and

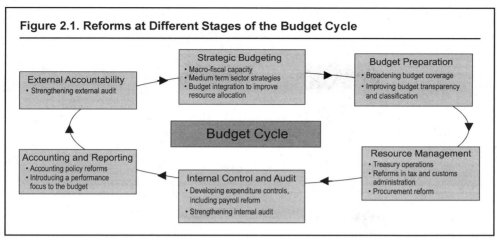

Figure 2.1. Reforms at Different Stages of the Budget Cycle

Source: World Bank.

medium term expenditures, while components of treasury reforms are considered under treasury operations, expenditure controls, and accounting policy reforms. A similar situation applies with the reform of the legislative framework for PFM. Rather than consider legislative issues as a separate component, legislative reforms are included where relevant in the different categories. Conversely reforms in budget transparency that occur at a variety of stages in the budget cycle (for example budget documentation, in year financial reporting, and end of year financial statements) are considered in a single category.

For each of the six stages of the budget cycle the relevant PEFA scores are first reported, followed by an assessment of each of the reform areas relevant to this stage. For each reform area, the report sets out briefly the underlying objective of this type of reform before reviewing experience in different MENA economies. It then provides an assessment of what has worked and what has proven to be more challenging.

Strategic Budgeting

Table 2.1. Relevant PEFA Scores for Strategic Budgeting

	Algeria	Egypt Arab Rep.	Iraq	Jordan	Lebanon	Morocco	Syrian Arab Republic	Tunisia	West Bank & Gaza	Yemen, Rep.	Average score
Multi-year perspective in fiscal planning, expenditure policy and budgeting	NA	NA	1.33	3.33	NA	2.33	1.33	NA	1.00	2.33	1.94
Aggregate expenditure out-turn compared to original approved budget	NA	NA	1.00	4.00	NA	4.00	2.00	NA	3.00	1.00	2.50
Aggregate revenue out-turn compared to original approved budget	NA	NA	4.00	4.00	NA	4.00	3.00	NA	3.00	4.00	3.67

Source: World Bank.

Macro-Fiscal Capacity

Why Is the Reform Important? Having a unit in the Ministry of Finance to provide macroeconomic and fiscal (macro-fiscal) policy advice is important for good aggregate fiscal management. A key task of the unit would be to assist in developing a medium term fiscal framework (MTFF) for the preparation of the budget. The aim of an MTFF is to guide the preparation of the budget so that fiscal policy is consistent with the government's monetary and exchange rate policies and debt levels are kept sustainable. The unit can also monitor progress with budget execution and advise whether a change to the budget stance is warranted during the year.

What Is Happening in the Region? The Ministries of Finance in the region have traditionally not had a strong macro-fiscal capacity. To the extent that this capacity existed within government, it was within the planning ministry. It tended to focus on contributing to planning activities, such as a five year plan, or general economic forecasting.

In recent years Jordan, Egypt, Lebanon, and the Republic of Yemen have started to develop some capacity in the Ministry of Finance to provide macro-fiscal advice.[1] Initially, many of these units focused on monitoring taxes, and the work was geared towards preparing monthly reports on budget execution. These monthly reports tended to be exercises in data dissemination rather than analysis, but the generation of these reports has proven to be a useful tool to develop capacity in the units. The units have been less active in providing policy advice on fiscal management. This capability can be expected to expand as the capacity of the unit improves and more ministers look for this advice.

As the units increase their capacity, they have become more involved in budget preparation through developing an MTFF. In many economies, the links between the MTFF and the final budget is still not strong, and this will require further development before the reform can be considered successful.

To carry out their role effectively, these units need to recruit staff with good analytical skills. The public sector pay and conditions make it difficult to attract such staff. It is therefore not surprising that in some economies (for example, Egypt and Lebanon), the officials working on these issues are not serving under standard public sector terms and conditions. Even with these contracts, there will be a challenge to retain staff as they develop experience.

Where it has not been possible to recruit staff on special contracts, it has been necessary to tailor the work of the unit to the capabilities of the staff available. In particular, as discussed above, where staff have limited economic forecasting skills, the units have given priority to fiscal reporting and forecasting. The unit has relied on other institutions (such as the central bank) for the relevant macroeconomic data.

Assessment. The establishment of a macro-fiscal unit has become important, as Ministries of Finance have attempted to develop a MTFF to guide the preparation of the budget. The work is analytically demanding, and attracting suitable staff within standard civil service contracts has proven to be a challenge. By initially focusing on fiscal forecasting, many units have made progress in preparing an MTFF, although the link between this and the preparation of the budget needs to improve.

Medium-Term Perspective

Why Is the Reform Important? In fiscal management, the cost of a policy in the next year is not always a good indication of its costs over time. For example, capital expenditures on a new school in one year can lead to a need for additional operating expenditure in the future. Similarly, some expenditure is driven by demographic movements that can change substantially over time. While the legal focus is on the annual budget, it is recognized that governments need to understand and make provision for the expenditure implications of policies in the coming years (typically the next three years).[2] To be implemented effectively, this requires a "bottom up" assessment of the medium term cost of existing policy—or "forward estimates"—often as part of a MTEF reform.[3]

What Is Happening in the Region? A number of economies in the MENA region are attempting to develop forward estimates as part of MTEF reforms, but none has a functioning system at present. The work has generally been carried out through pilot projects in various sectors. This is the approach that is being followed in Jordan and Lebanon. The PEFA assessments indicate that the lack of a medium term focus continues to be a major weakness in the region.

The development of sectoral forward estimates as part of an MTEF is a very resource intensive reform. Economies with limited capacity for reform might well decide not to embark on this initiative—an approach taken by Iraq. Even Jordan has faced delay with the reform because senior management has been distracted by the other PFM reforms taking place.

One of the challenges with this reform has been ensuring that it is integrated with the core budget preparation process. In Morocco and Tunisia, which were the first economies in the region to attempt to develop medium term forward estimates, the exercise remains separate from the budget itself and is viewed more positively by sector ministries than the Ministry of Finance. Although the forward estimates beyond the budget year are not legally binding, they do provide sectoral ministries with additional confidence of future resources. Conversely, some Ministries of Finance view the forward estimates with suspicion—taking the view that they restrict the "flexibility" with which the Ministry of Finance can manage budget preparation in the future. This is a concern of the budget directorate in Morocco, which has avoided implementing the reforms fully because it fears being tied by the forward expenditure estimates.

Another challenge with the preparation of forward estimates is ensuring that they focus on both the recurrent and capital budgets. In economies where the two budgets are not well-integrated, this does not always happen. In Jordan, for example, the focus of the estimates is on projects and not sufficiently on recurrent expenditures. Identifying the future recurrent implications of current capital expenditure is one of the more important elements of forward estimates, but it is also important to identify changes in recurrent expenditure needs that are not directly linked to projects.

Assessment. The argument for developing sector based forward estimates to provide a medium term perspective is compelling, but this is a major reform and should only be initiated once more basic improvements to the PFM system have been completed. While there is merit in starting the reform by working with pilot sectors, it is critical that the Ministry of Finance is supportive and committed to using the output in budget preparation. It is also important that the forward estimates include recurrent expenditures as well as projects in order to have a comprehensive picture.

Budget Integration to Improve Resource Allocation

Why Is the Reform Important? By integrating the management of operating and capital expenditures in the budget, the quality of government expenditure can be improved. In dual budgeting systems, there are often inconsistencies between the two budgets. For example, insufficient resources may be made available to maintain investments once they are complete. More generally, with a dual approach to budgeting, the link between policy interventions and the budget is weakened. High level allocations for the investment or operating budgets are more important in determining the final budget allocations than an assessment of the right mix of operating and capital expenditures for the sector.[4]

What Is Happening in the Region? All economies in the region inherited systems of budget management that separated recurrent expenditure from capital expenditure, and many continue to have separate ministries managing the two budgets. In addition to the separation of responsibility for budget management at the central institutions, there is generally further fragmentation at the level of line ministries with separate finance and planning departments responsible for the two budgets. Although the dual budgeting system is a legacy from the colonial powers, it is ironic that neither Britain nor France currently operates a dual budget.

In several economies in the region, noticeably the Maghreb economies and more recently Syria, the management of the two budgets is under the Ministry of Finance. However, even with this institutional integration, the Ministry of Finance operates separate processes in preparing the two budgets. Algeria integrated the management of the two budgets within sectoral units in the budget department in 2008, in an attempt to unify the processes.

While it is possible that budget integration could be achieved without consolidating budget management in one ministry, in practice the transaction costs of managing this transition have proven to be an impediment to effective integration. Jordan is one of a number of economies in the region that has received on-going advice from the IMF and the World Bank to consolidate budget management within the Ministry of Finance to assist integration. While the advice appears to be accepted at a technical level, no change has occurred. In Lebanon, some argue that integrating the capital budget within the Ministry of Finance would concentrate too much power under one minister. At present, the capital budget is managed by a separate agency reporting to the Prime Minister. In these circumstances, unless there is a strong political will to overcome institutional resistance, efforts to achieve budget integration are unlikely to be successful.

One of the key challenges when shifting institutional responsibility for the management of the capital budget to the Ministry of Finance is to develop the necessary analytical capacity in the relevant MOF staff. In general, Ministries of Finance have tended to manage the recurrent budget through incremental changes to the prior period budget. Planning ministries have often developed a broader range of project appraisal skills and are more experienced at assessing how projects fit with sectoral strategies. The different capacity of the two institutions has been one reason why some donors have favored maintaining their relationship with the Ministry of Planning for donor financed capital expenditures. The reform in Syria presents an interesting case study. When the management of the investment budget in Syria was transferred from the State Planning Commission to the Ministry of Finance, it was expected that many of the staff would be transferred as well. In practice, many of the staff were reluctant to leave the State Planning

Commission, and this left the Ministry of Finance poorly equipped to manage its new responsibilities. In view of this, the Budget Department established a specialist unit to manage the investment budget. So while budget management has been consolidated at the Ministry of Finance, the procedures for the two budgets remain distinct.

While integration of budget management has proven difficult in the region, some of the economies have taken steps to integrate the presentation of the two budgets. For example, Algeria now has a unified budget presentation. The West Bank and Gaza also presented its 2009 budget on an integrated basis. This can be a useful first step towards more substantive budget integration.

The issue of budget integration will become more pressing as economies move to introduce a performance focus to budget management. It is an anathema to performance budgeting to have processes for managing the preparation of the budget based on the nature of the expenditure inputs. The same applies to the separation of management between planning and finance departments within a line ministry. In a performance budgeting environment, it will ultimately be important to reduce restrictions on the use of inputs, which would make the budget split redundant. Moreover, it will be important to have a single process for monitoring the sectoral ministry as part of the accountability framework.

Assessment. All economies in the region continue to have elements of dual budgeting. While some progress has been made to integrate the presentation of the budget, efforts to integrate other elements of budget management have largely been elusive. In economies with a separate planning ministry managing the capital budget, institutional resistance to consolidating the budget management processes has been a particular problem. Where consolidation of budget management within the Ministry of Finance does occur, one of the main challenges is to ensure that the Ministry has the necessary analytical capacity to oversee the capital budget. For this reason, the transition needs to be carefully planned.

Budget Preparation

Table 2.2. Relevant PEFA Scores for Budget Preparation

	Algeria	Egypt, Arab Rep.	Iraq	Jordan	Lebanon	Morocco	Syrian Arab Republic	Tunisia	West Bank & Gaza	Yemen, Rep.	Average score
Orderliness and participation in the annual budget process	NA	NA	2.00	3.33	NA	4.00	3.33	NA	2.33	4.00	3.17
Classification of the budget	NA	NA	2.00	4.00	NA	4.00	1.00	NA	1.00	2.00	2.33
Comprehensiveness of information included in budget documentation	NA	NA	1.00	4.00	NA	3.00	1.00	NA	3.00	4.00	2.67
Transparency of Inter-Governmental Fiscal Relations	NA	NA	1.00	3.33	NA	2.00	2.33	NA	1.33	4.00	2.33
Public Access to key fiscal information	NA	NA	1.00	3.00	NA	4.00	1.00	NA	2.00	2.00	2.17
Quality and timeliness of in-year budget reports	NA	NA	1.33	2.00	NA	3.33	1.33	NA	3.00	1.33	2.05
Quality and timeliness of annual financial statements	NA	NA	1.33	2.00	NA	1.33	2.00	NA	1.33	2.33	1.72

Source: World Bank.

Broadening Budget Coverage

Why Is the Reform Important? There are two key reasons for ensuring that the scope of the budget is broad. First, the budget is the main mechanism for accountability—of both the executive to parliament as well as within the executive. Because alternative accountability mechanisms are often not put in place, extra-budgetary expenditures are not subject to adequate oversight. In addition, the budget is the main instrument for fiscal management. When expenditure takes place outside the budget, it undermines the budget's effectiveness as a mechanism for fiscal control and a process for allocating resources to the government's highest priority areas.

What Is Happening in the Region? Limitations in the scope of the budget are a general problem in the region. In Algeria and Morocco, the budget is fragmented with numerous special treasury accounts outside the general budget—although in the case of Morocco, there is disclosure of the fiscal information relating to these special accounts in the budget documents. In Egypt, significant third party revenues and unused budget allocations have been used for extra-budgetary expenditure, while in Lebanon the coverage of projects financed by foreign donors has not been adequately captured in the budget. Although the PEFA assessments do not address this issue directly, the low scores for unreported government expenditure support the view that this is an area of weakness.

One of the challenges in extending the scope of the budget is that there are strong incentives for those benefiting from the current arrangements to resist the change. In Egypt, the Ministry of Finance attempted to rein in extra-budgetary expenditures as part of its treasury reform. While significant balances were initially brought back to the Central Bank of Egypt, these were kept separate from the government's main bank accounts, and the procedures for the management of the expenditures were not amended. Some of the balances later returned to commercial banks—effectively unwinding the initiative, although the IMF has recently reported that the reform is on track.

In Lebanon, the coverage of foreign financed projects in the budget was considered a delicate political issue, as the current arrangement gives the Prime Minister considerable influence over these expenditures. In 2007, a budget law was drafted allowing for the integration of the largest extra-budgetary entities into the budget—although this was only to the extent of the aggregate flows. However, the law is yet to pass. It failed to address the extra-budgetary expenditure of other large entities, such as those providing health services; family allowances and pensions; and financing to the economy's 927 municipalities.

The technical demands of extending budget scope and coverage are not significant, and good progress can be made where there is the political commitment. For example, in Jordan, a number of steps have been taken to extend the coverage of the budget, and the PEFA assessment indicates that only a small proportion of total expenditures are not covered. However, there needs to be a strategic approach taken to these reforms which anticipates the likely resistance from vested interests.

Assessment. Improving budget coverage is important to promote accountability for government expenditure and to support the effective allocation of resources. While the technical demands are not significant, improving the coverage of the budget has proven to be difficult for many economies in the region. There are strong vested interests in the existing arrangements, and this is a reform that requires firm political commitment if it is to be successful.

Improving Budget Transparency and Classification

Why Is the Reform Important? The need for better information on budgeted expenditures is one element of a general trend towards improved budget transparency in developed economies. This reflects the view that greater transparency in budget documents can play an important role in building the credibility of the government's fiscal policy with the public, parliament and external financiers. Reforming the budget classification is an important component of this broader objective. Traditional budget classifications have tended to mix expenditures of different economic nature, and it was often difficult to obtain a clear understanding of what was happening with the government's accounts.

What Is Happening in the Region? Many economies in the region are reforming the economic classification used in the budget to align with the classification used in the IMF's Government Financial Statistics (GFS) 2001.[5] This change has recently been made in Egypt, the Republic of Yemen, and Iraq, while Tunisia is developing a new classification for use in 2015. Morocco has a budget classification that is broadly consistent with GFS, while Lebanon has had a classification aligned with the earlier GFS 1986 since the late 1990s. Both Algeria and Syria have developed a new economic classification based on the GFS 2001 but have yet to implement it. The improvements in economic classification are reflected in relatively high PEFA scores for the quality of budget classification for a number of economies.

While many of the above economies focused solely on the economic classification, Jordan has taken a more comprehensive approach and developed a new chart of accounts as part of its Government Financial Management Information System (GFMIS) project. This includes a revised economic classification in line with GFS 2001, along with new administrative, functional, fund and geographic classifications.

There are reports that the changes to the economic classification have substantially improved the quality of fiscal information in some economies. The benefits of changes to the administrative classification are not as obvious, but are also important as they can improve the accountability for budget allocations. As the administrative classification is also often used to approximate the purpose of expenditure (function), it can be very important in improving the quality of information for policy makers.

It has been common for those providing technical assistance in the PFM area (particularly the IMF) to help economies prepare a new economic classification. Once the classification is updated, its use tends to become embedded within the PFM system and the reform becomes enduring and self-sustaining. However, a major investment is required to train staff during the transition. In Iraq, the training on the new classification system was viewed by some as inadequate, and this has reduced the quality of information produced.

In addition to reforming the budget classification, many MENA economies have taken steps to improve the transparency of budget reporting. One sign of these improvements is that the *Open Budget Index* recently improved Egypt's ranking from near the bottom (a rating of "provides scant to no information") towards the middle ("provides some information")—a significant improvement from 2006 to 2008.[6] Tunisia prepares well documented and easy to understand budget documents, although only with a one year horizon. Jordan's budget documents meet almost all information benchmarks required by transparent practice, one omission being a list of financial assets. In Morocco and Algeria, the documents are extensive, although there are important gaps and the information is not always user friendly. For example, in Algeria there is a lot of general information but no fiscal balance, no information on public corporations and no information on contingent liabilities. The Republic of Yemen, Iraq, and West Bank and Gaza have also increased the information content of their budget documents—again with some gaps.

Another important initiative has been to provide monthly reports on budget execution during the year. This is now happening in Morocco, Egypt, Jordan, West Bank and Gaza and Lebanon. These reports are generally posted on the relevant Ministry of Finance website. The PEFA scores for this subcategory reflect some progress in this area, although the overall performance is mixed.

There are some specific features of this reform that have helped to make it successful. First, the preparation of the information is generally carried out by a small number of staff within the Ministry of Finance. As such, it is easier for technical assistance to initiate the work and for these changes to be maintained. Second, as the reports are prepared on a frequent cycle, they become part of the routine of the relevant staff. In West Bank and Gaza, it has become a source of pride for the Ministry of Finance staff that the reports are always prepared by the 15th of the following month—which is reflected in their relatively high PEFA score. Finally, while increased transparency can be a powerful tool, there are likely to be fewer vested interests opposed to the presentation of specific information.

Assessment. There has in general been good progress in improving the quality of budget classification and the transparency of budget documents. After initial technical assistance, the budget classification reforms in particular have been enduring once the change was introduced. Similarly, monthly reporting and improvements to the transparency of budget documents has often been enduring. This is in part because the reforms rely on a small team of staff in the Ministry of Finance for implementation, which makes them better placed to succeed in an environment where the civil service has limited capacity. Moreover, because the reforms are considered technical, they have tended to meet less opposition from vested interests than many other PFM reforms.

Resource Management

Table 2.3. Relevant PEFA Scores for Resource Management

	Algeria	Egypt, Arab Rep.	Iraq	Jordan	Lebanon	Morocco	Syrian Arab Republic	Tunisia	West Bank & Gaza	Yemen, Rep.	Average score
Predictability in the availability of funds for commitment of expenditures	NA	NA	2.33	4.00	NA	2.33	1.33	NA	1.33	1.33	2.11
Recording and management of cash balances, debt and guarantees	NA	NA	2.00	3.33	NA	4.00	2.33	NA	2.00	3.33	2.83
Transparency of taxpayer obligations and liabilities	NA	NA	3.00	3.00	NA	4.00	NA	NA	NA	3.00	3.25
Effectiveness of measures for taxpayer registration and tax assessment	NA	NA	2.00	2.33	NA	3.33	NA	NA	NA	3.00	2.67
Effectiveness in collection of tax payments	NA	NA	1.33	3.00	NA	3.33	NA	NA	NA	1.33	2.25
Competition, value for money and controls in procurement	NA	NA	1.33	3.00	NA	3.00	1.00	NA	NA	1.33	1.93

Source: World Bank.

Treasury Operations

Why Is the Reform Important? A well functioning treasury system can reduce the cost and risk of government operations.[7] In particular, it can improve cash management and minimize thegovernment's net borrowing costs. By consolidating cash holdings, it can also reduce the government's exposure to the risk of bank default.

What Is Happening in the Region? A number of the economies in the region have embarked on treasury reforms to improve cash management. While progress has been made, the reforms have not always been implemented as originally envisaged.

In general, the reforms have involved establishing a treasury single account (TSA) at the central bank, with a series of transaction accounts holding "zero balances" at commercial banks. This arrangement allows cash to be consolidated in an account at the central bank while utilizing commercial banks for branch network operations. When fully developed, the reforms involve active cash planning to understand the cash needs of the government so that the consolidated cash balances can be managed on a daily basis. Although the reform should also be associated with steps to improve debt management, few economies in the region have made progress in this area.

Improving cash management by moving towards a TSA has been part of the reform agenda in Iraq since at least 2005. In that year, a joint World Bank/IMF mission recommended, as a medium-term reform (that is, by the end of 2006) that progress towards TSA should be made, subject to improvements in the payments and banking systems.[8] Progress has been limited and, in 2008, the IMF reported that the GoI did not yet operate a TSA and continued to hold large idle balances outside the main treasury account.

In Jordan, while many of the bank accounts were initially consolidated at the central bank, a number of accounts were not consolidated and outside the capital Amman, positive cash balances continued to be held at commercial banks. After some delay, it appears that agreement has now been reached to consolidate most of these balances—although in spite of this, a recent IMF/World Bank report noted that government deposits with commercial banks had recently increased. Lebanon also consolidated some balances at the central bank, but a number of important accounts were kept separate and the balances in these accounts were not available to meet cash needs. These limitations were not in general technical but more to do with whether the Ministry of Finance had the authority to consolidate the balances.

As discussed earlier, a similar issue arose in Egypt. The Ministry of Finance attempted to close a large number of accounts at commercial banks in order to consolidate the government's cash balances. However, facing vested interest from the "owner" of the account, the balances were kept separate within the central bank and eventually many returned to commercial bank accounts. The IMF has recently reported a fresh initiative by the Ministry of Finance on this reform.

In the Republic of Yemen, it was proposed to establish a treasury in the Ministry of Finance to assume many of the budget execution functions at present carried out by the central bank. The reform has not progressed, in part because it was dependent on the implementation of the new information system (AFMIS), which has taken far longer than initially anticipated to make fully operational. More generally, there was limited enthusiasm from the Ministry of Finance for the reform and considerable unease from the central bank, which at present has 80 percent of its staff involved in supporting the budget execution function.

The use of cash plans for active cash management is at an early stage for economies in the region. Good progress has been made with cash planning in Jordan, but this remains a "research exercise" and cash management is still mainly through cash rationing. In Lebanon, cash rationing is still being used on a daily basis by the Ministry of Finance to decide which bills to clear. A start has been made to prepare a cash plan to guide budget execution, but there has been reluctance to involve line ministries in the preparation of the plan, which limits its status and has raised questions about whether the Ministry of Finance is truly interested in making this reform.

Cash constraints are also a significant problem in the West Bank and Gaza. However, there is an interest in moving to a more systematic arrangement and a cash plan was developed for 2009 with input from line ministries. The reform is in its early stages, and the cash plan is not yet being used to assist cash management.

It is worth mentioning that in economies with cash rationing in effect, the Ministry of Finance has considerable influence. It is therefore not uncommon to find the MOF less than enthusiastic about moving to a more systematic cash management system.

With treasury reforms there are a number of technical challenges, and a lot to learn from the experiences of other economies. For this reason, it is valuable to have technical assistance to support the reform. However, a greater need is to have solid commitment from staff within the Ministry of Finance for the reform. While other PFM reforms can be managed by a small team within the Ministry of Finance, these reforms affect many administrative employees throughout the public sector. Unless there is strong leadership from senior staff at the Ministry of Finance, the changes are difficult to implement successfully.

Assessment. While some progress has been made on treasury reforms in the region, this remains work in progress. Although a TSA has been established in many economies, the coverage is often not complete because the Ministry of Finance has not had the authority to consolidate some balances. A number of economies have set up units to prepare and maintain a cash plan, which can assist in aligning the borrowing and investment activity with the government's cash needs. However, too often the cash plans are not being actively used in cash management. Few economies have taken steps to improve debt management systems as part of treasury reforms.

Reforms in Tax and Customs Administration

Why Is the Reform Important? The collection of tax and customs revenues involves a number of challenges. Although the government collects tax by exerting its coercive power, this will meet strong resistance from taxpayers if the system is not perceived to be fair and efficient.[9] By improving the administration of the tax system, government can increase the revenues it collects consistent with the applicable laws, while enhancing the fairness of the system and reducing the compliance costs for taxpayers. The latter is important, as complying with the tax system can be a high cost of doing business.

What Is Happening in the Region? In general, the MENA economies have made much better progress with tax administration reform than they have with expenditure reforms. Historically, economies in the MENA region have had a low tax to GDP ratio and inefficient tax systems that gave considerable discretion to the tax inspectors. Many economies are now interested in increasing the taxes collected—pressed to do so in some cases by the prospect of declining oil revenues. In light of this objective, a number of Ministers of Finance have taken an active interest in reforms to improve tax policy and administration. An additional motivation has been to improve the business environment.

There are some impressive achievements in tax administration reform from the region. Egypt has made considerable progress from a low starting point, and a 2008 IMF report noted a variety of important accomplishments. They include: (1) the successful implementation of self-assessment for income tax; (2) the creation of the Egyptian Tax Authority, as a vehicle for tax administration modernization; and (3) the establishment of a large taxpayer center and a pilot medium-size taxpayer center in Cairo. These reforms are at an early stage but the progress to dates is impressive.

Jordan amalgamated the income and sales tax units into a new tax authority, and more recently it has made a number of changes so that the tax system provides an attractive and stimulating environment for local and international investors. In this regard, they conducted a comprehensive review of tax regimes to simplify and reduce their number to a minimum and consolidated the legislation. Morocco is considered to have a good tax system with a clear legal basis. A single taxpayer identification number is under development, and performance criteria for tax audits have been adopted. The introduction of large and medium taxpayer offices as "one stop shops" for taxpayers has also been adopted in Lebanon and Algeria, while the Republic of Yemen has also introduced a system of self assessment for large companies.

It is interesting that more progress seems to be made on revenue administration issues than on expenditure administration. There are a number of possible explanations. One interesting observation is that it has been possible in some economies to provide real incentives to staff of the tax authority as part of the reforms. In particular:

■ While in the past, tax administration was often just another department in the Ministry of Finance, many of the reforms have set up a separate tax authority or at least introduced separate administrative arrangements for the tax department. In Lebanon, this approach has allowed otherwise restrictive civil service wage rates to be bypassed. Being a tax official is a sought after job within the administration. Syria is also putting emphasis on this approach as part of its tax reforms.

■ A number of economies in the region have also established bonus arrangements to provide tax collectors with an additional incentive. Tunisia attributed part of a recent increase in its tax collections to changes to the bonus structure.

Providing incentives for staff has been more difficult for expenditure reforms because of the wider implications for government administration. These incentives have had a positive effect in helping establish a new culture for tax administration. On the other hand, such arrangements have led some of the better staff to move from expenditure roles within government, exacerbating existing capacity problems in these areas. For this reason, caution should be exercised in deciding whether to adopt the approach.

Assessment. Tax administration reforms have in general been more successful than expenditure reforms in the MENA region. In part, this is because Ministers of Finance have taken an active interest in the reforms. However, tax administration is also a distinct function within government and it has been possible to support reforms by introducing separate administrative arrangements to provide stronger incentives for staff. One unhelpful consequence of this tactic has been that some of the better staff have moved to tax administration from expenditure roles within government, exacerbating existing capacity problems in these areas. For this reason, caution should be exercised in deciding whether to introduce incentives for tax administration in isolation.

Procurement Reform

Why Is the Reform Important? The way in which the purchase of goods and services is controlled through the procurement process can help the government to minimize collusion, kick-backs and other corrupt practices. Improvements to procurement procedures can therefore lower the cost of government expenditures.

What Is Happening in the Region? As can be seen in the PEFA scores, many MENA economies have weak procurement systems. The Republic of Yemen provides a good example of the type of problems that exist. The external audit body has commented that the procurement system is rife with fake competition, abuse of contract variations with subsequent project overruns, non transparent tender evaluations, an all too frequent resort to direct procurement methods, and the use of "slicing" to bypass procurement and authorization thresholds.

Procurement reforms are being discussed in a number of economies, usually on the back of a new procurement law. This is the approach being followed in the Republic of Yemen and West Bank and Gaza. A new law has also been drafted in Lebanon, but is awaiting approval by the Council of Ministers before it can be submitted to parliament. In all cases the new laws include:

- establishing an independent public procurement agency under the new procurement law
- preparing standard bidding documents based on the new law
- preparing a user's manual and guidelines.

Procurement reforms have taken time to implement. the Republic of Yemen has been working on the reform for over five years and has been actively supported first by the World Bank, and more recently with training by USAID. Syria developed a new law in 2005, but this contained a number of weaknesses and the World Bank is now supporting work to revise the law. The delays stem from a variety of factors, but an important element is the strong opposition to reform from individuals and institutions benefiting from the existing system. In many cases, this is due to significant elements of corruption in the government procurement system.

Assessment. The quality of procurement systems in the region is weak. Reforms have been attempted in a range of economies, but the timescales for these reforms have been extended and the outcomes have been disappointing. The reforms often touch on areas of significant corruption and therefore can pose a threat to particular interests which have strong incentive to delay or divert the process. The failure to make progress in large part reflects an unwillingness to confront these special interests.

Internal Control and Audit

Table 2.4. Relevant PEFA Scores for Scope of Budget

	Algeria	Egypt, Arab Rep.	Iraq	Jordan	Lebanon	Morocco	Syrian Arab Republic	Tunisia	West Bank & Gaza	Yemen, Rep.	Average score
Composition of expenditure out-turn compared to original approved budget	NA	NA	2.00	1.00	NA	2.00	1.00	NA	2.00	2.00	1.67
Stock and monitoring of expenditure payment arrears	NA	NA	1.00	1.00	NA	2.33	NA	NA	1.33	-	1.42
Effectiveness of payroll controls	NA	NA	1.33	3.00	NA	3.33	1.33	NA	2.33	1.33	2.11
Effectiveness of internal controls for non-salary expenditure	NA	NA	1.33	3.00	NA	2.33	3.33	NA	1.33	1.33	2.11
Effectiveness of internal audit	NA	NA	1.33	2.00	NA	2.33	2.33	NA	2.00	1.33	1.89

Source: World Bank.

Developing Expenditure Controls

Why Is the Reform Important? It is an obvious point, but effective expenditure controls are important to ensure that expenditures remain within the budget allocations and support aggregate fiscal control; as well as that the budget's role in allocating resources to sectoral expenditures occurs in a timely manner at the lowest cost, and that any changes in circumstances during the year can be accommodated. In addition to general expenditure controls, there are specific requirements to manage effectively the payroll procurement process. Because of the link to the transaction cycle, the controls are an important element in addressing corruption associated with government expenditure.

What Is Happening in the Region? The economies in the region tend to have extensive and time-consuming control systems, but these systems are often not effective. As can be seen in the PEFA scores, controls on payrolls and non-salary expenditures, as well as the management of arrears, are all areas of weakness. The composition of the outturn also differs greatly from the approved budget in all economies.

In order to improve the quality of expenditure control, reform proposals are being made to:

■ streamline the control processes and clarify accountability
■ apply controls at the point of commitment
■ improve the quality of controls on procurement and payroll.

It is common practice in the region to have multiple signatures associated with the clearance of each transaction. Where there are numerous signatories to a given expenditure, it is often not clear who is ultimately responsible and hence accountable for misuse. This can be problematic within one institution, but in economies like Lebanon, Syria, Jordan, and Morocco the problem is exacerbated by having a range of different agencies involved in the ex ante control process. In addition to weakening accountability, the procedures can become a major impediment to the government's ability to conduct business. In a number of economies (notably Iraq), the delays caused by heavy control procedures are said to explain delays in capital projects. Moreover, in Lebanon, the problem is used as a rationale for managing capital projects outside the government system.

Despite the problems being faced in the region, there have been relatively few attempts to date to streamline the control procedures. Morocco has embarked on a reform of the organization of its ex ante control system. In 2006, the *separate bodies that control* payment orders and commitments were merged. In 2007, cumbersome virement rules were revised to provide greater flexibility to ministries. This has already resulted in improvement in the timeliness of budget execution. It is also planned that "ministerial treasuries" will perform a simplified modernized ex ante control, which will be based on risk assessments and the size of the transactions. However, few of these treasuries have been established. There have been proposals to streamline the ex ante controls system in Lebanon, but the latest reform action plan makes only a marginal mention of this initiative. The lack of focus on this issue is in part a reflection that the need for reform is not accepted. However, it is also recognition that the reform would be challenging, given it would involve changing the roles of some institutions.[10]

Cash rationing and the build-up of arrears is a major problem for many of the economies in the region. Lebanon, West Bank and Gaza, the Republic of Yemen, and to a lesser extent Egypt and Jordan have identified problems with expenditure arrears.[11] While many of the problems stem from the poor quality of budget preparation, there are opportunities to better manage the problem if expenditure controls are exercised at the point of expenditure commitment. At present, many economies implement the expenditure controls at the point of payment, by which time the liability has been created and the only question is when payment will be made. In Lebanon, there is an additional complication posed by the violation of the annuality principle in the regular budget.

To address the arrears problem, Morocco has introduced a system of commitment controls, although the draft PEFA assessment suggests that the system is not yet working effectively. West Bank and Gaza is in the early stages of introducing commitment controls in conjunction with the new accounting system. The recent IMF/World Bank mission to Jordan has recommended that commitment controls also be a feature of the financial management system being developed. On the other hand, while a commitment control feature is part of the software specifications in the Republic of Yemen financial management information system, this functionality has not yet been designed or activated. Although it is possible to implement commitment controls in the absence of computerization, all the reforms to date are progressing as a component of an IT project.

The PEFA scores suggest that, in relative terms, the management of payrolls is in better shape than other expenditure controls. Both Jordan and Morocco have solid scores in managing the payroll. Progress on a more limited basis has been made in Lebanon. Overall payroll controls in Egypt are fairly effective as payroll audits are carried out, though they are not comprehensive. Lebanon's computerization of payroll and pension management in the 1990s was a major achievement. In 2006, the MOF introduced direct computerized bank payment to public sector employees, which has also allowed a reduction in the number of ghost workers.

Payroll reform is a particular priority in West Bank and Gaza and the Republic of Yemen—although the problem in each economy is different. In the Republic of Yemen, the problem is one of ghost workers and double dippers, while in West Bank and Gaza it is the lack of budget discipline in the recruitment process. In West Bank and Gaza, payroll controls have improved substantially in 2007 and 2008. They provide more assurance on the integrity of an item that in the 2009 budget constitutes more than 60 percent of recurrent expenditure. In particular, the payroll system is now connected with the accounting system of the MOF, and a separate financial controllers department reviews the payroll on a monthly basis.

In the Republic of Yemen, a civil service project started in 1998 which included the establishment of a clean personnel database by 2001. The project was restarted in 2005 with a re-visitation of the clean up exercise (principally of double dippers and ghosts) through a new database that includes biometric control data. However, the clean up exercise currently covers around 70 percent of all Government employees and does not include a significant portion of the ministries of Defense and Internal Affairs. There is a consensus among knowledgeable observers that the former is likely to be particularly problematic in terms of ghost workers and double-dippers. Furthermore, the biometric system is not as of yet closely linked to the payroll, which does not allow it to function as intended.

Assessment. The quality of expenditure controls in all forms is poor for economies in the region. Despite the problems being faced, there have been few attempts to date to streamline and strengthen the expenditure control procedures. Where the reforms involve institutional changes, they have proven particularly challenging. Progress has been made by some economies in payroll management, but this is uneven. The overall impression is that where there is a failure to make progress, it is mainly due to a lack of genuine interest in the reforms.

Strengthening Internal Audit

Why Is the Reform Important? Internal audit aims at providing the executive with assurance of the quality of the financial management systems—in particular the implementation of financial controls and the management of risks.[12] Depending on the system of control in place, this could be assurance to the Ministry of Finance or to the senior management of the line ministry.

What Is Happening in the Region? The PEFA assessments indicate that the internal audit function is poorly developed in most economies in the region, with Morocco being one of the few economies to have a relatively positive PEFA assessment. Many of the weaknesses are similar to those found with the external audit bodies and relate to problems of the scope of work carried out, concerns about conflict of interest, and institutional clarity.

In many economies, the internal audit function has a strong transaction focus, and aims to identify cases of mismanagement or a failure to follow procedures rather than looking at the adequacy of the overall systems. This is often a feature where the function has emerged from a Soviet style inspection service. The internal audit in Syria is an example of this, and the relatively strong PEFA assessment for Syria reflects the extensive control which is applied through this system rather than the adequacy of the scope of its activities. In economies such as Lebanon and Jordan, internal audit is part of the ex ante control process. This compromises the auditor's independence, as any assessment is a comment on the auditor's own work. Institutional clarity is a particular problem in Tunisia where there are several internal audit bodies, with one reporting to the Prime

What Is Happening in the Region? The idea of focusing on performance has been around for some time, but in the last twenty years many OECD economies have re-formed their budgets to introduce a more explicit performance focus. Such reforms have been given different labels — with program, output, or results oriented budgeting being among the most common.

In view of the broader global trend towards improved effectiveness in public administration, there is considerable interest from economies in the region in introducing a performance focus to the budget. The earliest efforts were made by Jordan, which started its results oriented budgeting reform in 1998. In recent years, a number of other economies have started to work on pilots for program based budgets, including Morocco, Algeria, Tunisia, Lebanon, and Syria.

The Jordanian experience is particularly instructive. The first efforts were supported by the German aid agency GTZ and continued from 1998 to 2004. They were ultimately considered too ambitious and had little impact. Since then, an approach has been piloted in the Ministry of Education and is being extended to other ministries. Initially, there appeared to be little ownership of this initiative by the General Budget Directorate of the MOF, but this is no longer the case. A recent review by the IMF/World Bank noted that progress has been made. However, it also commented that the reform has not yet delivered the benefits that were expected. One reason identified is that the lack of some basic elements of the PFM system (for example, commitment controls) has tended to negate the progress with this more advanced reform.

Morocco has also been working on performance budgeting reforms for a number of years. The World Bank provided assistance to the government to develop a performance budgeting approach, based on pilots in a number of ministries. However, while some performance budget documents were drafted, government support for this exercise was weak and the initiative has not been pursued after these initial drafts. More recently, the MTEF reform is being used to develop more performance focus. A methodology was developed in 2006 and work on the MTEFs has continued, but to date the budget is an input based document.

Tunisia has four results based budgeting pilots underway with support of the World Bank, but it is taking a measured approach to the reform. The intention is to include the pilot ministry information as an annex to the 2011 budget. A similar path is being followed by Syria, although it expects to include some material on its two pilots in the 2010 budget. A European Union project financed training and study tours for staff in the Syrian Ministry of Finance over a number of years, but there was no reform to the budget as a result of this initiative. The latest developments are taking place in a low key fashion with the support of the IMF. In Algeria, a pilot program budgeting was carried out in FY07. It was not repeated in 2008 but is expected to resume in 2009. Full adoption of program budgeting and management is planned for the budget in 2012, if the new organic budget framework law is adapted by parliament in time.

In West Bank and Gaza, a pilot approach was rejected and all ministries were asked to develop programs to establish a link between the budget and the government's reform plan.[15] The program structure was used for presentation purposes in the 2009 budget, although it will be refined in future years. One of the motivations for this reform has been to demonstrate that budget support from donors is being used as planned.

The slow progress on introducing a performance based approach is in large part because it is necessary to have many of the basic elements of the PFM system in place before it can work effectively. Often these weaknesses are only fully recognized when work on a pilot begins. Prominent examples of the challenges facing reforms in this area include the following:

- In Syria, the work with pilot ministries revealed that—in addition to the standard dual budgeting problem—a large portion of sectoral expenditure (say in education or agriculture) is fragmented between the relevant sector ministry and the Ministry of Local Administration. Unless this institutional fragmentation can be addressed, it will hamper the efforts to make program budgeting effective.
- In the West Bank and Gaza, it was recognized that the accounting systems need to be adapted to allow programs to be monitored during the execution of the budget. While chart of accounts changes are manageable, the accounting system will not be able to manage complex cost allocations. This will mean that some of the programs initially defined will need to be simplified to meet the capacity of the accounting system.

Another challenge is to avoid the reform becoming an information collation exercise, which loses sight of the objectives. When fully developed, a program structure can involve a range of sub-programs and activities. Combined with associated performance indicators, the information demands can be extensive. This might make sense in a well-developed budget system where skilled staff are able to effectively use the information. However, in an environment where there are capacity constraints in both preparing and using the information, the data collation process can become an end in itself, undermining the reform. This was a criticism of initial work on results oriented budgeting in Jordan. Also, the budget documents in Morocco include hundreds of input or output indicators, but little attention is paid to them. The government intends to improve these performance indicators, including reducing their number.

Finally, it is worth noting that Egypt, the Republic of Yemen, and Iraq have decided not to start work on a performance focused approach to budgeting at this point. In Iraq in particular, this reflects recognition that there are more fundamental reforms deserving priority.

Assessment. There is considerable interest from MENA economies in introducing a performance focused approach to budgeting. However, the successes are limited to date and the timeframe for the reform is proving to be extended. This reform is complicated and difficult—in part because it relies on having many other elements of the PFM system functioning at a reasonable standard. For this reason, even where the reform proceeds, every effort should be made to avoid conceptually sophisticated approaches and to ensure that the approach can be supported by the accounting systems.

External Accountability

Table 2.6. Relevant PEFA Scores for External Accountability

	Algeria	Egypt, Arab Rep.	Iraq	Jordan	Lebanon	Morocco	Syrian Arab Republic	Tunisia	West Bank & Gaza	Yemen, Rep.	Average score
Scope, nature and follow-up of external audit	NA	NA	-	2.00	NA	1.33	2.33	NA	1.00	3.33	2.00
Legislative scrutiny of the annual budget law	NA	NA	1.00	4.00	NA	3.33	2.33	NA	2.33	2.33	2.55
Legislative scrutiny of external audit reports	NA	NA	1.00	2.00	NA	1.33	1.33	NA	1.00	1.33	1.33

Source: World Bank.

Strengthening External Audit

Why Is the Reform Important? External audit provides parliament with assurance on the adherence to financial laws, the reliability of the financial statements, and value for money in government expenditure. As such, it provides an essential discipline on the financial management of the executive.

What Is Happening in the Region? The PEFA assessments indicate that the external audit functions of economies in the region have a range of weaknesses. Egypt is an extreme example as the activities of the Central Audit Organization, which is Egypt's Supreme Audit Institution, are shrouded in secrecy. In Algeria, the last published annual report from the National Audit Court was in 1996–97, and its reports are not now publicly available despite an apparent requirement that they be published in full or in part in the Official Gazette.

With some economies, the weaknesses relate to institutional problems, with many external audit bodies reporting to the President or King instead of solely to the parliament.[16] In many economies, the audit function has a strong transaction focus, with the aim of identifying cases of mismanagement or a failure to follow procedures rather than looking at the adequacy of the overall systems. In economies such as Lebanon and Jordan, external audit is involved in ex ante control, compromising the auditor's independence. In Tunisia, a good quality external audit is carried out by the Court of Accounts and the INTOSAI standards on autonomy, scope, and quality are met. However the value of audit work is limited by the fact that it is only partially published, the public accounts may be some two years old by the time the settlement law is considered by parliament and by the lack of any formal parliamentary hearing on the report by the Court of Accounts on this act. A similar situation applies in Morocco.

In spite of the weaknesses in the external audit bodies, there appear to have been relatively few efforts to reform the external audit functions. Given the relatively limited role played by the parliament in most of the economies in the region, it is not surprising that there is limited demand by the parliament for support in holding the executive to account. This is reflected in the very low PEFA scores for legislative scrutiny of audit reports for all economies in the study.

Although there are proposals for future reform in Jordan and Lebanon, the three economies with the most experience with audit reforms to date are Iraq, West Bank

Gaza and the Republic of Yemen. They have had mixed experiences. In Iraq, the reform involved introducing a new inspector general function based on the U.S. model. A number of PFM experts believe that this reform has not been successful, as the new function is not well understood and is not integrated with the existing oversight institutions. The change has also exacerbated existing capacity problems.

In West Bank and Gaza, a new audit body was established in 2005. However, in light of the prevailing political instability during that period, the capacity building process restarted in 2007. It has received little technical assistance from donors to date, but a major capacity building project is about to start financed by the European Union. Alongside this project, the external audit is being guided by the Auditor General of Norway for the audit of the 2008 financial statements. This would be the first audit of financial statements since 2003. The audit is not complete, but the early indications are that working through a "live" audit will be a very productive capacity building exercise. The presence of the Norwegians has also provided the external audit with needed credibility in its discussions with the Ministry of Finance. The extensive effort made by the Ministry to document and support the 2008 accounts has also confirmed the vital role that an external review can play in ensuring discipline in the financial management function. Without the possibility of external review a range of sloppy—if not unethical—practices can easily develop.

In the Republic of Yemen, the external audit body has received support from GTZ for a number of years. Since 2007, the body can be seen to be having a real influence, with active consideration of its report by the parliament. Before then little progress was apparent. Although the project has been active since 2005, the reform towards an institution meeting INTOSAI standards is still work in progress. For example, only now has a draft audit bill been completed and forwarded to the President to address (among other things) the independence of the external audit agency.

Assessment. Most economies in the region have weak external audit functions, in part reflecting the relatively minor role played by parliaments in many economies in the region. While the focus of external audit is on providing assurance to parliament, the presence of an effective audit body can also support reforms in budget execution by encouraging more discipline in the accounting practices. However, ultimately the success of efforts to build the capacity of the audit body will depend on whether the parliament is prepared to utilize the auditor's report.

Notes

1. Although in Lebanon's case, it was led by consultants outside the Ministry of Finance.
2. Taking a medium-term perspective also helps avoid ad hoc and across-the-board expenditure cuts when fiscal adjustment is required, as it recognizes the value of targeted savings that take time to bear fruit.
3. The term MTEF is generally used to refer to a group of budget reforms—including the development of a Medium Term Fiscal Framework (MTFF), which is considered as part of the macro-fiscal section above.
4. While the term capital budget is used in this report, the nonrecurrent budget is variously referred to as the capital, investment, or development budget by economies in the region.
5. While the GFS 2001 is an accrual system, these economies are generally using the classification while following cash-based accounting.
6. See http://www.openbudgetindex.org/.

7. Treasury reforms are often used to refer to a range of PFM reforms relating to budget execution. These can include cash management, expenditure control, and accounting reforms (often in an improved IT environment). In this section, the focus is on cash management reforms.

8. In fact, the Financial Management Law (CPA Order 93 of 2004) requires that all receipts shall be credited to a Treasury Consolidated Account and paid into the Treasury Single Account, and all payments shall be debited to the Treasury Consolidated Account and withdrawn from the Treasury Single Account.

9. This analysis focuses on the administration of general government taxes and duties related to income, trade and consumption, and so forth. Where economies rely on revenues from petroleum or other natural resources, a different set of challenges apply.

10. This can be particularly problematic where there are known to be side payments for staff associated with the expenditure control process.

11. In Algeria, funds release is not timely and arrears do develop, but the petroleum revenues have been available to finance any arrears that emerge.

12. While internal audit can also provide comment on the value for money of expenditures, this is not generally a core function.

13. A third body has a particular focus on public property issues.

14. In this section the focus is on accounting methodology and standards.

15. Palestinian National Authority, *The Palestinian Reform and Development Plan* (PRDP), 2008.

16. Whether joint reporting is in practice a problem depends on whether the arrangements compromise the willingness of the auditor to raise concerns or problems.

CHAPTER 3

Implementing Reforms in Public Financial Management: An Emerging Set of Promising Practices in MENA?

One of the lessons of public finance reform is that people do not 'eat' reform, people cannot relate to reform. So what is important is to look for ways to make people actually feel the difference.

Salam Fayyad

At one level, it is an admittedly artificial exercise to separate the content of reforms from their implementation, for the two are inextricably linked. The nature of the reforms being implemented will inevitably influence the pace and timing of change, the size of the effort, and the actors engaged in it. Yet the science (or art) of management has also long-realized that the way in which reforms are implemented can have an important impact upon their realization. This chapter seeks to review the lessons that have been learned from a decade or more of trying to implement public financial management (PFM) reform in the Middle East and North Africa (MENA) region to understand if there are obvious pitfalls to be avoided or approaches that will elevate the prospects for success. It also seeks to better understand the various political and bureaucratic dynamics surrounding these changes.

How Important Is Implementation to the Success of MENA's PFM Reforms?

Before proceeding, it is important to better understand the role of implementation in contributing to successful PFM reforms. As table 3.1 indicates, not all reforms are created equal. This table breaks the MENA experience with PFM reform down along three dimensions. The first category are reforms that have typically been "more successful," in that a number of MENA economies have been able to implement them effectively and achieve concrete, independently verifiable improvements. The third category, "challenging PFM reforms," is comprised of reforms that have shown themselves historically to be more difficult and problematic. It does not mean that they have been impossible to implement, and some MENA economies may have been able to put in place certain elements of these reforms. But this is not common. The "mixed" category represents an area where generalizations across the region are difficult to make and the results are often more specific and unique to a given economy.

Table 3.1. Breakdown of Successful and Challenging PFM Reforms in MENA

Successful PFM Reforms	Mixed	Challenging PFM Reforms
• Improving budget classification • Improving budget transparency • Reforms in tax and customs	• Enhance macro-fiscal capacity • Budget integration • Streamlining ex ante control processes • Commitment control • Payroll management • Treasury operations • Reform of accounting systems • Internal and external audit	• Medium term sector strategies • Improving budget scope and coverage • Introducing performance into the budget • Procurement reforms • Large information technology projects

Source: World Bank.

Two types of PFM reforms have been particularly successful in MENA: efforts to improve budget transparency and classification, and revenue related reforms, particularly those involving the reform of tax and customs. Ironically, these represent two very different types of reforms. The first are relatively straightforward and technocratic in nature. An existing body of accepted practice exists to reform economic classification, in the form of the IMF's 2001 *Government Finance Statistics Manual* (GFSM), and there are incentives to align accounts along standard international practice to facilitate the production of comparable fiscal and economic data. While there may be some resistance to such reforms stemming from basic bureaucratic inertia, no fundamental interests are challenged or mandates threatened. Once implementation is complete, the reform becomes part of the fabric of the system and endures. It is therefore not surprising that many MENA governments have been able to take this step.

This is not true for revenue consolidation or reforms in tax and customs, where the stakes are much higher. Revenue agencies are often among the entities in government where problems of corruption are most pronounced, since their function places them in a position to extract rents and "facilitation payments" in exchange for a variety of favors. Efforts to restructure and reorganize such functions often encounter fierce resistance from both those on the inside (who benefit from informal payments) and some on the outside (who have learned to work around the current system and use it to their advantage). Such reforms are not for the timid or hesitant.

Yet if the challenges are great, the gains are often significant as well. For governments facing significant fiscal deficits, it is often more politically palatable to raise revenues—difficult as that may be—than to engage in painful cuts in expenditure. In Lebanon, for example, reforms in tax policy and administration were initiated since the 1990s because it was the largest single source of revenue for the government. A combination of tax and customs reforms, including moving to a VAT, was able to increase government revenue by US$1.88 billion between 1997 and 2003, or from 11 to 16 percent of GDP. In Egypt, reforms in tax policy and administration implemented in 2005 and beyond brought over 1 million new taxpayers into the system and increased income tax revenue from 7 to 9 percent of GDP. Beyond the promise of new revenue, such reforms are often initiated to remove obstacles to increased private investment. For all of these reasons, such reforms are able to garner the requisite high-level political support to see them through in spite of considerable opposition.

Unfortunately, on the other side of the spectrum are a host of reforms that are neither particularly easy to implement nor which bring the promise of substantial fiscal gains, at least in the short-term. Some, such as improving the scope and comprehensiveness of the budget, are not technically difficult to implement. Progress has been made in a number of settings, such as Jordan and the West Bank and Gaza. However, the political hurdles are considerable, as many powerful entrenched interests often prefer to remain off-budget. Unless significant political capital is invested in overcoming such resistance, these reforms are unlikely to move forward.

Other reforms, such as the development of MTEFs, introducing large information and communication technology (ITC) projects and integrating more performance information into the budget, are often both technically demanding and run up against powerful vested interests. In many cases, their successful implementation may depend upon underlying systems, procedures, and practices being in place that may not exist. It is therefore not surprising that their implementation is frequently delayed or halted. As one assessment of PFM reforms in the Republic of Yemen noted with refreshing candor, "for the Finance Minister or the National Public Financial Management [Reform] Coordinator, only those set of reforms which can bring instant recognition and resources to the government are of priority...reforms which are painstaking and long-term without immediate benefits take a back seat."[1]

Under such circumstances, it may be tempting to conclude that—in the final calculation—it is the nature of the reforms themselves as much as the way they are implemented that is responsible for their ultimate success or failure. In the words of Egypt's Minister of Finance, Youssef Boutros Ghali, "it is easy to change laws—it is hard to change the attitudes of those who implement them."[2] Reforms that are largely technical in nature will be easier to implement; those that are technically demanding and rely upon certain preconditions to be in place will be more difficult. Reforms that do not alienate powerful constituencies will be easier to implement; those that cross fundamental political and bureaucratic interests will be more difficult. Reforms that have a high payoff in terms of tangible, concrete returns in the near term will be easier to implement; those whose benefits are more distant or ephemeral will not be.

While there is certainly truth in this contention, reality is more complex and nuanced. Considerations of political will, leadership talent, the broader authorizing environment, and internal capacity (to name but a few) can shape and modify reform agendas in ways that confound simple predictions. Few would have anticipated that Salam Fayyad, for example, would have enjoyed the success that he has in reforming West Bank and Gaza's PFM practices. His initial focus on consolidating banking arrangements, strengthening expenditure controls and budget reforms—while desperately needed—would not have been areas that held great promise for far-reaching improvements on an a priori basis. In a similar fashion, one would have expected that some of the higher income economies with more effective administrations would have been able to make greater progress towards strengthening internal and external audit than has been the case so far. There are a few cases where poorly designed interventions have been made to work through shear dogged determination, albeit often with compromises in timing, cost, and functionality. There are far more in which reforms that were generally sound and appropriate floundered through poor implementation.

for the obvious reason that, prior to the revolutions of 2011, elections themselves were typically less important.

Of more relevance are cabinet reshufflings. Their impact upon PFM reform agendas can be extraordinarily difficult to predict, but at a minimum such changes are disruptive and can reduce the incentive to support reforms with long gestation periods. This is particularly true in economies where cabinet turnover is more frequent, such as Jordan, where the average life span of a government between 1999 and 2007 was six to eight months. During this period, the Hashemite Kingdom has witnessed no fewer than eight Ministers of Public Sector Development portfolio and five Ministers of Finance. The implications for reform were spelled out in the words of one former civil servant:

> It took three months to convince a new minister about our objectives, mandate, and by the time the person understood, he left. So much of our efforts were directed to educating ministers. Ministers knew that their tenure was short lived and that they would not stay for more than one year, and it affected the program greatly. They were interested in short term wins instead of longer term reforms and seeing the process in a holistic manner.[6]

Syria provides an interesting study in contrasts. Prior to the recent outbreak of unrest, the two key reformers for PFM (the Deputy Prime Minister and the Minister of Finance) have had continuity in their positions, which has helped to facilitate Syria's reform efforts. However the broader geopolitical developments in the period have exerted tremendous pressure on Syria and diverted some attention of the key political figures.

It is difficult to determine if context is a definitive factor affecting PFM reform in MENA or merely an important one. If reforms are largely technical in nature, have a solid rationale behind them, are supported by well-positioned champions within the relevant ministries, and if they avoid alienating powerful constituencies, then under most circumstances they can probably stay "under the radar screen" and survive the shifting political, economic and administrative sands. Lebanon was able to implement some important reforms in payroll management, for example, even in the midst of a chronic political crisis and the absence of a functioning parliament.

But Lebanon's experience is also instructive, in that when these reforms have needed to move beyond the realm of what could be implemented by a Ministry of Finance decree and required broader cabinet or parliamentary approval, they have stalled. There are no examples of more far-reaching PFM reforms that came to fruition if the broader political context was not supportive. Nor are there examples of where senior officials were able to isolate and protect major PFM reforms from major shifts in the broader political climate. Put succinctly, an ebbing tide grounds all large boats—regardless of how well they are designed or the skill and determination of the captain.

Lesson 4: The Wisdom of "Muddling Through"— Grand Strategy versus Incremental Change

To what extent are MENA PFM reform agendas driven by an overarching strategic framework or integrated plan, versus a more flexible and improvised approach that seeks to take advantage of opportunities when they emerge?

The answer is not entirely straightforward. On the one hand, MENA does not suffer from an absence of strategic plans for upgrading systems and procedures. Algeria drafted a PFM reform strategy in 2007, which has yet to be formally approved, although its Organic Budget Law articulates the directions of reform. In a similar fashion, Egypt has drafted a PFM strategy in 2008 which is currently under consideration by the MOF. Jordan had a Strategy for Financial Reform from 2004-2007 that was also embedded in broader national reform plans, including the *National Agenda*. In Morocco, PFM reforms have been embedded with the Governments Public Administration Reform Program of 2003. In Tunisia, a PFM reform program is being implemented and improving the use of resources as component of the Strategy for the Development of the Public Service 2007-11. The Bank has been assisting the Tunisians in drafting a budget reform master plan in 2008, which has not yet been formally approved but was used by the government in negotiating budget support from the EU. The Palestinians have clarified their intentions for PFM reform in a variety of documents, such as *Building a Palestinian State: Towards Peace and Prosperity*, which was presented to donors in Paris in December 2007. The Republic of Yemen's PFM reform strategy was approved by Cabinet in 2005 and has also been supported by the donor community.

Furthermore, there have been examples of when economies would have benefited from adopting a more comprehensive approach to PFM reform. Egypt has attempted a wide range of PFM reforms, for example. However, beyond the realm of tax and customs, progress has generally tended to be patchy and of limited duration. Until recently, there has been no overarching strategic framework within which reforms have been planned, prioritized, sequenced, costed, evaluated for feasibility, and monitored. In a similar fashion, prior to 2008, Iraq's management of the PFM reform process has suffered from the absence of any overall vision, strategy, or prioritized and logically sequenced action plan. For example, the many capacity building workshops that have been run in and outside Iraq have provided participants with new knowledge and skills, but this training has tended to be ad-hoc and provided without the benefit of a more comprehensive framework for staff development, which in turn should be grounded in a careful assessment of the functions that the various ministries should be performing and the skills required to do them well. The lack of a more comprehensive approach can be particularly problematic in the development of integrated financial management information systems, as will be discussed in greater detail below.

Such reform strategies can be valuable as a statement of intent, or for communicating priorities, securing donor support, or providing political cover for a given set of activities. Yet their role in actually shaping successful reforms can be modest. The development of such plans is no guarantee that they will be implemented expeditiously. In many MENA economies, roll-out has taken much longer than expected, with a number of components being dropped or modified along the way.

Nor are such plans a prerequisite for success. Egypt's far-reaching reforms in tax and customs were initiated in 2004, yet its broader plan for PFM reform is still under review. Senior officials repeatedly emphasized the probing and opportunistic nature of these reforms, while underscoring that the general strategic direction was clear. Salam Fayyad adopted a flexible view to West Bank and Gaza's PFM reforms, recognizing that he could not determine *a priori* the sequencing of reforms or expect to have control over the entire process.

He explains:

> The context in which you are operating has to be kept in mind all the
> time. It's not easy. You are working within a system of deeply en-
> trenched habits—not good ones—so you basically have one of two
> choices. Either to come in and say, 'this is what I want to do. Either
> it's done, or I'm out,' which is what everyone was expecting, or maybe
> even banking on. Or, you could be opportunistic: do what you can, as
> soon as you can do it, wherever you can do it. I chose the latter way…
> But, at all times have clarity as to what is important and what is not too
> important.[7]

Fayyad describes his approach as being, "patient, deliberate, methodical, and opportunistic, looking for an opening here and there." It was informed by a clear set of
priorities. He began by focusing on the major structural problems related to revenue and
expenditure management, treasury systems and the budget, which he described as "elements without which you cannot have a well functioning public finance system." But
he combined this strategic orientation with tactical flexibility in terms of the sequencing
and timing of reforms. His Deputy Finance Minister, Jihad al Wazir, notes that the actual
sequencing of the West Bank and Gaza's PFM reform agenda was heavily influenced by
political dynamics, and based on doing "what you can get done at the time."

In the final analysis, the optimal approach is likely to be one of "strategic opportunism." Such an approach would combine careful upstream analysis of the major strengths
and weaknesses confronting a given PFM system, perhaps drawing upon a variety of
analytic tools such as PEFA, PERs, CFAAs, CPARs, Fiscal ROSCs and the like, in forming
a clear set of strategic objectives. But it would realize that there is an inherently organic
nature to reform that makes it unlikely to proceed in a rational, linear fashion. Within
MENA, the most effective reformers are those who have been strategic in recognizing
and selecting appropriate windows of opportunity, while being flexible and opportunistic in exploiting them.

Lesson 5: Establish Basic Systems before
Contemplating More Advanced Reforms

The temptation is often irresistible for governments and international advisors to strive
for quantum improvements in performance by adopting some cutting-edge practices
from OECD economies into a developing economy context. More often than not, the result has been a litany of dashed expectations and failed reforms. In response, the Bank's
Public Expenditure Management Handbook (1998) emphasizes the importance of "getting
the basics" right before moving on to tackle more advance reforms. Drawing upon earlier work by Alan Schick and others, a number of precepts have been laid for doing so.[8]
This list includes:

- foster an environment that supports and demands performance before introducing performance or outcome budgeting;
- control inputs before seeking to control outputs;
- account for cash before accounting for accruals;
- establish external controls before introducing internal control;
- establish internal control before introducing managerial accountability;

- operate a reliable accounting system before installing an integrated financial management system;
- budget for work to be done before budgeting for results to be achieved;
- enforce formal contracts in the market sector before introducing performance contracts in the public sector;
- have effective financial auditing before moving to performance auditing
- adopt and implement predictable budgets before insisting that managers efficiently use the resources entrusted to them;

The PFM reform experience within MENA largely bears this out. This has been particularly true with regard to two sets of initiatives that have been among the more technically advanced to be implemented to the region: the move to a Medium Term Expenditure Framework, and the effort to introduce greater performance orientation into the budget process. Both have shown themselves to be complicated and problematic to implement, in part because their realization has relied upon a number of preconditions to be in place before they can be effective, and in part because senior officials have been generally unwilling to allow themselves to be bound by such initiatives.

As the discussion in Chapter 2 indicates, a number of economies in MENA have sought to implement MTEFs, including Algeria, Jordan, Lebanon, Morocco, and Tunisia. None have implemented such a system in its entirety. Jordan has probably made the most progress in implementing several components of an effective MTEF, although these reforms are still in their early stages. Other economies have made significantly less progress. Lebanon's MTEF is only a general guidance to sectors communicated in the budget circular in the form of an overall budget ceiling. The MTEF is operational only as a pilot project in the Ministry of Education, and even there it only sets ceilings in terms of overall expenditure. In Morocco, an MTEF methodological guide was developed on preparing sector MTEFs in 2006. This guide has been approved and transmitted officially to line ministries by circular of the Prime Minister in 2007. In 2008, nine sector/ministry MTEFs were prepared, and MTEFs for five additional ministries are now underway. However integration with the budget has yet to be achieved and, at the moment, preparation of the budget remains input based with little explicit discussion of policies and priorities.

In a similar fashion, reforms to introduce a greater focus on performance into the budget have often taken a long time to implement and been hindered by the lack of underlying conditions, such as a well-functioning accounting system that can yield accurate cost data. Such efforts can be prone to delays and interruptions. With regard to Algeria, for example, the performance budgeting pilots were stopped for one year by the MOF, and real ownership of the MTEF and performance budgeting pilots by the line ministries may be questionable. Jordan has also begun experimenting with some elements of performance budgeting, although the effort is still in its infancy with pilots being carried out in a few ministries. An earlier performance budgeting initiative assisted by GTZ Germany from 1999 to 2004 was regarded as being too ambitious and had little impact.

In some respects, a more interesting question is whether it makes sense to hold out objectives such as MTEFs and performance budgeting as a distant goal in the hope of gaining traction on some important but more pedestrian reforms, such as improving budget classification or upgrading the ability of the accounting system to provide more accurate cost data. A case could be made that embedding these smaller and "less glam-orous" reforms in a broader objective will give them greater visibility and cohesiveness than they would otherwise enjoy. While such an approach cannot be ruled out entirely, MENA's experience demonstrates that—while it may help with the initial "marketing" of the reform package—it is not a recipe for long-term success. It is better to set modest, measureable objectives and achieve them than goals that, with the passage of time, ap-pear more and more ambitious and unrealistic.

Lesson 6: When Possible, Keep Reforms Quick, Simple and Mutually Reinforcing

It is an accepted article of faith among many officials and development practitioners that major PFM reforms are difficult, complex undertakings that require years or sometimes decades to fully reach fruition. Laws and regulations must be drafted; longstanding practices restructured; political and administrative cultures changed; institutions built and capacities strengthened. To attempt such undertakings quickly, so the argument goes, is a recipe for poorly thought through implementation and eventual failure.

As with many managerial maxims, there is some truth to these contentions. PFM reforms in a number of MENA economies, such as introducing MTEFs or greater perfor-mance orientation into the budget, introducing major IT systems, improving the quality of expenditure controls, or strengthening internal and external audit capacity do take a long time to implement. Algeria's Budget System Modernization Project began in 2001 and was finally closed in 2009 after its objectives had been significantly scaled down. Morocco's PFM reform agenda has been moving forward gradually since 2003. Reforms in West Bank and Gaza have been underway since 2002.

Yet there are also cases where reforms can be implemented quite quickly when the requisite political will exists. Reforms in expanding the scope and comprehensiveness of the budget, for example, can be implemented within weeks or months if the proper political will is in place. Reforms in improving budget transparency can also be imple-mented within no more than a month or two.

Furthermore, some of the more effective reforms were deliberately implemented with haste. Salam Fayyad wanted to generate confidence in the reform agenda by taking specific, quick steps that made an impression. He explains, "I have learned about the need to move fast, and make an impression. It gets more difficult with time, not easier. You need to use your success as a stepping stone. Success breeds success. If you say 'give me time, I will assess,' that is the wrong approach. You need to immediately begin to make an impression."[9] These sentiments were echoed by Youssef Boutros Ghali, who notes, "the faster you move, the less resistance you will encounter, because it takes time for your opposition to organize and mobilize."[10]

The reality of MENA's experience is that many PFM reform efforts, including those of both Fayyad and Boutros Ghali, tend to follow an uneven trajectory. Periods of re-form and progress are offset by intervals of limited activity and little forward movement. Sometimes, these periods of inactivity can be extensive. (Relatively little happened in Algeria's PFM reform effort, for example, for nearly five years.) Admonitions to move with haste can help maintain momentum and push agendas forward. Otherwise, as has happened far too often in MENA, reform can become "business as usual" and lose any sense of priority or urgency.

The Use of Pilots. A related question is whether to pilot reforms or roll them out whole. In MENA, pilot PFM reforms have been implemented in a wide variety of contexts. Algeria piloted some reforms in program budgeting but then discontinued the exercise. Egypt piloted the creation of a medium-size taxpayer unit in Cairo and the introduction of reduced ex ante controls over virement in three governorates. Jordan piloted a results-based budgeting exercise in the education sector. Lebanon has piloted the introduction of internal audit within the Ministry of Finance. Morocco has also sought to pilot performance budgeting in a number of ministries. In the 2010 budget, Syria piloted the introduction of a program structure that integrated recurrent and investment budgets in two pilot ministries. Tunisia is piloting program budgeting in four ministries. Information systems have been piloted in a number of economies, including Jordan and the Republic of Yemen.

The jury is still out regarding the effectiveness of pilots. Not surprisingly, the answer to this question is likely to be highly contextual and dependent upon both the nature of the reform and the institutional context in which it is being rolled out. On the positive side, pilots—particularly when combined with rigorous monitoring—provide an opportunity to gain valuable experience in identifying potential problems that could plague a particular set of PFM reforms and rectifying them before too much damage is done. This is particularly important when the roll-out is likely to be time-consuming and expensive, as is the case with large IT systems.

However, in the absence of firm commitment to proceed with a particular set of reforms, pilots can often become an opportunity for delay and inaction. Line departments in many MENA economies are often unenthusiastic about pilots, preferring to adopt a "wait and see" approach rather than invest time and energy implementing new approaches that may ultimately not be implemented. It is interesting to note that, after initially intending to pilot the introduction of the MTEF in specified ministries, Jordan's General Budget Department decided to roll out forward estimates and performance indicators to all ministries rather than starting with a number of pilots. They did so with the understanding that it will take time to build depth in the process and bring about more fundamental changes in budget planning processes, but the effort was worthwhile and needed to proceed regardless. Furthermore, pilots tend to do better in administrations with a history of experimentation and innovation than those with fixed traditions embedded in a strong legal framework. In the Algerian context, for example, it can be easier to implement top down reforms based on laws and regulations rather than those that involve studies and pilots.

The Value of "Virtuous Circles." Finally, certain sets of reforms can foster "virtuous circles" and positive feedback loops, whereas others require constant effort. Budget classification is an example of the former, and it is not surprising that it has been one of the more effective reforms of its type in MENA. While it requires effort in overcoming institutional inertia and capacity building, once these skills have been obtained, it becomes easier each year to prepare and implement the budget with the new classification scheme. Other examples are reforms to the payment processes, payroll procedures, and monthly reporting. Once introduced, these procedures have continued. Even when there was a break in monthly reporting in the West Bank and Gaza during the Hamas period, for example, such reforms were reinitiated without too much difficulty.

Lesson 7: Be Wary of Large Financial Management Information Systems

An integrated financial management information system (IFMIS) can offer great benefits for all PFM activities, especially budget execution. Such systems can facilitate timely and accurate reporting; allow internal controls to be exercised through the IFMIS, and therefore support more consistent compliance; and allow central agencies to oversee budget execution by line ministries, therefore facilitating the devolution of responsibility to front line managers while retaining information at the center. All economies in the region have made some effort to introduce computerized systems to support PFM. In general, two different strategies have been taken towards this reform. These are to develop either: (1) a "sophisticated" fully integrated IFMIS; or (2) a simple customized IT system to support budget execution. While there are some small successes to date, the "sophisticated" projects have been problematic.

The fully integrated IFMIS approach has been followed by the Republic of Yemen, Iraq, Egypt, Syria and more recently Jordan. Although the first efforts started in the Republic of Yemen in 2003, as of 2010 none of the systems are fully operational. The Jordanian GFMIS—which was financed from local resources—appears to be best placed for successful implementation. In contrast to the other projects, the Jordanian GFMIS appears to have followed sound project management procedures and had active involvement from staff in the Ministry of Finance.

At the other end of the spectrum were efforts by USAID and a U.S. consulting firm, Bearing Point, to implement a Freebalance system in Iraq. As the discussion in box 3.2 indicates, work began in implementing this system in 2003. After spending nearly US$30 million in developing the system, USAID suspended work on the project in June 2007 and eventually signed an MOU with the Ministry of Finance handing over full ownership. While efforts continue to implement the system, recent assessments indicate that it is being used only for a modest number of government transactions.

While the Iraq project used an off-the-shelf package, the Yemeni project was customized to meet local demands. Neither is considered to be particularly successful, although the Yemeni system is likely to meet the basic functionality required by the government. In Syria, the IFMIS was developed as part of an EU project with limited involvement of line staff in the Ministry of Finance. The system was completed in 2008, but there is no indication from the Ministry of Finance that it is ready to be used. In Egypt two separate systems (AGES and IFMIS) were being developed in parallel by different teams. While the IMF recommended that the AGES project be discontinued, for some time the IFMIS was also not promising. However, a number of the problems appear to have been addressed, and recent assessments by the IMF suggest that the development of a new computerized financial management information system, under a project being managed by Booz Allen, is well on track.

The second approach has been to develop simple computerized systems with limited functionality to help support budget execution. The systems are usually customized to fit the specific needs of the budget execution system of the economy. This approach was followed by Lebanon in the late 1990s and the system is still in place. More recently in West Bank and Gaza a simple system was developed, which in the space of four months went from concept to managing payments.

The use of a simple system has advantages—especially in cases such as West Bank and Gaza, where a new budget execution system was needed at short order. They tend

---

Box 3.2. History of the Iraq IFMIS System

In 2003, the Coalition Provisional Authority (CPA) instructed USAID to begin implementation of the Iraq Financial Management Information System (IFMIS) through a contract implemented by the consulting firm BearingPoint. This task was undertaken to modernize Iraq's public financial management systems within a cash accounting framework. It was a key component of Iraq's stand-by agreement with the IMF.

By June 2007, the IFMIS had been rolled out in 132 spending units (SU) nationwide. According to Bearing Point and the MOF, these 132 SUs collectively accounted for over 80 percent of GOI expenditures. Work on the IFMIS was terminated by USAID following the abduction of five Bearing Point consultants in May 2007 at the MOF, as well as due to difficulties in aligning the system to the needs of the Iraqi government.

On January 14, 2008, USAID and the Ministry of Finance (MOF) signed a Memorandum of Understanding (MOU), which gave impetus for USAID to restart the program by outlining an agreement to cooperatively identify and resolve technical issues and transfer full ownership of the IFMIS to the MOF. While USAID may continue to offer limited technical assistance to the MOF to operate, maintain, and update the system, the MOF will assume full ownership of the computer hardware and software.

However, questions remain about the extent to which the system is truly being utilized. As of January 2009, eleven pilot SUs have been using IFMIS for less than five months and entered an average of less than 10 percent of total monthly transactions during the period of July to November 2008.[a] A World Bank assessment of this experience noted that it had been plagued by a number of problems, including:

- unsatisfactory project supervision and contract management arrangements
- lack of support for and recognition of Project Management Teams
- insufficient or inappropriate incentives to promote the Government's PFM reform agenda
- inadequate consultative, coordination and co-financing arrangements to support high levels of ownership, effective partnerships and high degrees of commitment from key stakeholders
- poor FMIS design and more specifically the planning process to set the FMIS implementation strategy
- the absence of a medium-term PFM reform program that informs the prioritization and sequencing of specific PFM reform measures including development and roll-out of an FMIS.

Source: World Bank.
Note: a. This discussion is adapted from USAID, Iraq Financial Management Information System Assessment, (January 2009), http://pdf.usaid.gov/pdf_docs/PNADO270.pdf.

---

to have much lower initial development costs and, provided their objectives remain minimal, they may also be an efficient way of exposing officials only familiar with paper based operations to the potential of a future IFMIS. However, there are limitations to the approach. First, because the systems are developed to order, they often do not include standard functionality that has proven to be useful in other systems. Second, the systems tend to be less flexible in dealing with new user requirements than off the shelf systems. This is a problem with the Lebanese system, where changes to the budget procedures can require substantial reprogramming of the IT system. While the initial cost of the system may not have been high, these costs increase over time as the system is reconfigured for new developments. For these reasons, the use of a simple system should be seen as a short term solution, with the eventual aim of moving to a fully integrated system. As with any short term solution, it is important to avoid overinvesting in developments that will eventually be superseded.

In summary, all economies in the region have been undertaking some IT investment to support the PFM system, but the record of the large projects in particular is not successful. There are a number of problems that have undermined these large projects, but two important concerns are: (1) weak project management arrangements; and (2) inadequate commitment and/or engagement of staff of the Ministry of Finance to the reform. The alternative of developing a simple non-integrated system to order has been successful in some economies in the short term. In general this approach makes sense as a step towards eventually developing an IFMIS, but not as a long term solution in its own right.

It should be noted that MENA's experience with FMIS is hardly unique. In both the public and private sectors, the implementation of large IT systems has often been problematic. In one study, fully 75 percent of IT systems implemented in the United States failed to fully deliver in terms of their time, cost or projected functionality. Other studies have cited similar failure rates. The reasons for this lack of success are many. On the design side, they include insufficient analysis of the business case; poor definition of project scope and objectives; insufficient time allotted and over-optimistic planning. Project management issues include insufficient backing from senior executives; a lack of authority or decision-making ability in the team; poor collaboration and communication; and inadequate tracking and reporting. Even under the best of circumstances, large IT systems can be complex and difficult to implement. A World Bank study in 2003, for example, noted that a review of Bank FMIS projects took on average over seven years to complete with an average cost of US$12.3 million. Thus the problems that large IT systems encounter in MENA are more likely to reflect the difficulties inherent in implementing such systems anywhere, particularly in low capacity environments, rather than any special technical or administrative challenges unique to the region.

Lesson 8: Internal Challenges: Leadership, Coordination, Skills, and Incentives

MENA's reform experience holds a number of important lessons as to how such reforms should be structured and organized. This section addresses several key themes, including: (1) the stature and status of key reformers; (2) the coordination of PFM reforms within government; (3) how reform units and project management units have been structured; (4) their staffing and skills mix; and (5) the role of the chief executive. Each is discussed in detail below.

Stature and Status of Key Reformers. It is axiomatic in the literature of public management that reforms need to have a champion. It is therefore not surprising that many of the most far reaching PFM reforms within MENA have been driven by powerful ministers of finance, who play a uniquely important role in taking the PFM reform agenda forward. There is, quite simply put, no more important position for advancing this agenda in the region.

In this regard, the experience of Salam Fayyad in the West Bank and Gaza and Youssef Boutros Ghali in Egypt is particularly instructive. Both men brought a combination of impressive expertise and solid technical understanding of the issues. Their backgrounds are remarkably similar—both have PhDs in economics and spent time in the International Monetary Fund before assuming their duties. Beyond technical knowledge, they brought managerial talent and dynamism, along with a clear vision as to what needed to be done and considerable political savvy. Perhaps most importantly, they brought sheer determination. As Boutros Ghali notes, "you need to be fixated—single minded—and repeat yourself over and over again until it happens."[11]

Egypt's experience is also instructive, in that major reforms cannot be implemented by the Minister alone. Boutros Ghali argued that he could not do a tenth of what was needed. He needed a group of like-minded reformers around him, around 50 in his estimation, to help take the reforms in tax and customs forward. Part of their responsibility was to provide the necessary technical expertise when needed; part of it was to oversee the implementation of various dimensions of the reform agenda; and part was to monitor if actions were being taken as promised. The question of how to best balance external and internal expertise is a thorny one that will be addressed in greater detail below. However, in the view of Minister Boutros Ghali, such a cadre of committed in-house allies was essential, as one should not underestimate the tenacity of resistance to major reforms from the rank and file bureaucracy.

Coordination of PFM Reforms within Government. While national legal and institutional frameworks differ at their core, PFM reforms center upon the Ministry of Finance. The MOF has clear responsibility for the recurrent budget in all of the economies in this study, and MOF staff seconded to line departments play an essential role in authorizing expenditure. The extent to which the MOF dominates the budget and expenditure process may vary. In a few administrative contexts, the MOF is clearly the dominant player in most aspects of public financial management; in others, it has historically played more of an instrumental role in facilitating and monitoring decisions taken elsewhere. Jordan is unique in that responsibility for formulating the recurrent budget has been given to a quasi-independent agency, the General Budget Directorate, with a weak reporting relationship with the Ministry of Finance. Regardless of these arrangements, the MOF occupies a pivotal position in the reform of public finances, and no PFM reforms in MENA have been able to move forward unless the ministry is fully on board and committed.

Most economies also have powerful Ministries of Planning who look after the capital budget. In a number of economies, such as Jordan, West Bank and Gaza and the Republic of Yemen, the Ministry of Planning is responsible for issues of donor coordination. However, a few (such as Egypt) have given this function to other agencies, such as the Ministry of International Cooperation. Many also have various supreme audit agencies or *cour des comptes* who play a role in ex-post (and occasionally ex ante) audit and approval. Beyond the immediate core actors, there are a wide array of public sector participants and stakeholders in the budget process, including ministries, agencies, departments, commissions, deconcentrated and subnational entities, and state owned enterprises.

The quality of coordination between these agencies and the MOF varies both within and between economies, but it is frequently problematic and occasionally dysfunctional. Iraq serves as an example of the latter. One of the most significant challenges facing the GoI is to improve the integration of the capital and recurrent budgeting processes. Bank analysis of the Iraqi PFM system found that reforming these arrangements will be challenging owing to the traditional rivalry between the two ministries, the political allegiances of the respective ministers and the need to ensure no loss of face on the part of either ministry. A 2006 assessment of Algeria's PFM reforms also noted lack of inter-agency coordination and a failure to adequately engage with line ministries as a

Unfortunately, even when successful, PFM reforms do not translate readily into political gains. In the January 2006 elections to the Palestine Legislative Council, Salam Fayyad's "Third Way Party" received 2.4 percent of the popular vote and won only two of the Council's 132 seats. There are examples when the public has actively opposed various aspects of the reform agenda, such as when Egyptian pharmacists called a nationwide strike and took to the street in protest against a decision by the Ministry of Finance to alter retroactively a previously agreed arrangement as a part of the tax reforms.

Lesson 10: Lessons for Donors: Be More Strategic, Selective, Modest, and Flexible

The donor community has been heavily, although unevenly, engaged in providing support to public financial management reforms throughout the MENA region. Those most involved include the International Monetary Fund, the World Bank, the OECD, UNDP, and the European Union. A number of bilateral donors are also heavily engaged in providing support, including Britain's Department for International Development, the United States Agency for International Development, the *Agence Française de Développement*, and the Dutch and Norwegian governments, among others.

A detailed assessment of the effectiveness of donor funding is beyond the scope of this exercise, which has focused more generally on the PFM reform challenges confronting the economies of the MENA region; the types of reforms being implemented; and which have shown promise to date and which have not. Nevertheless, a few conclusions emerge that may be valuable to donors active in this area. They are discussed below under three headings: (1) the nature and scope of donor engagement in MENA on PFM issues; (2) the substantive lessons for donors regarding PFM reform; and (3) modalities and processes.

The Nature and Scope of Donor Engagement in MENA on PFM Issues. Table 3.2 provides a breakdown of average donor support for PFM issues by economy drawn from the OECD DAC database. Approximately 10 MENA economies received donor assistance for PFM reforms during the period from 2003 to 2007, with the lion's share going to Iraq, Morocco, and Jordan. Other recipients included Algeria, Egypt, Lebanon, Syria, Tunisia, West Bank and Gaza, and the Republic of Yemen. According to OECD DAC figures, total funding for PFM was around US$459 million during this five year period. The average was US$92 million, with considerable variation between years.

While the data probably provides a rough proxy for relative levels of donor engagement, care should be taken to not read too much into the findings, since some of these figures may reflect budget support with a PFM focus rather than dedicated resources for PFM reform. The latter is likely to be much more modest, probably averaging in the US$1 to US$5 million dollar range per economy annually after adjusting for the odd major IT project, with some economies receiving substantially less. The bottom line is that PFM reform in MENA is not an area where the donor community has over-invested.

It is hard to make judgments regarding the effectiveness of this assistance. An effort to see if there was any statistical relationship between levels of donor aid for PFM and PEFA scores among recipients turned up virtually no correlation whatsoever (the R^2 coefficient is 0.00).[15] The implications of this finding are unclear. It could mean that donors have not been effective in their support for PFM operations. Far more likely, it means that they allocate their assistance for PFM reform on criteria other than the underlying performance (or lack thereof) of the recipient economy, as measured by the PEFA indicators.

Table 3.2. Donor Support for PFM Reforms in MENA

PFM-ODA commitments (current US$ million)	2003	2004	2005	2006	2007	(Partial) total per economy	Annual average
Iraq		0.04	..	137.61	40.20	177.85	35.57
Morocco			0.00	100.86	0.24	101.10	20.22
Jordan	0.01	2.38	0.04	25.48	58.51	86.42	17.28
Tunisia	0.43	0.48	0.13	..	41.39	42.43	8.49
West Bank and Gaza	11.54	2.62	4.12	1.35	3.10	22.73	4.55
Syria		9.94	0.39	..	0.00	10.33	2.07
Egypt		0.02	1.02	3.78	6.23	11.05	2.21
Yemen, Rep.	0.19	0.04	1.86	..	3.99	6.08	1.22
Algeria			0.17	0.28	0.26	0.71	0.14
Lebanon					0.20	0.20	0.04
Total for MENA	**12.17**	**15.52**	**7.73**	**269.36**	**154.12**	**458.90**	**91.78**

Source: OECD DAC. Data are for the most recent years available.
Note: .. = Negligible.

In all likelihood, the influence of donors over the PFM reform process is more subtle and nuanced than can be captured by simple correlations. Donors can be a powerful impetus for change and reform, although their "persuasiveness" is closely aligned with a given economy's level of aid dependence. In economies such as Algeria and Syria, where donors have relatively little influence on government decision-making, domestic political and internal dynamics predominate. Donors can play a role in proffering advice and disseminating information, but government's enjoy great discretion over whether they choose to accept this advice or not. In settings such as the West Bank and Gaza and the Republic of Yemen, where governments are heavily aid dependent, donors are able to play a more influential role in pressing for various reforms. A much less powerful but still important factor is the role of the international community. In the Maghreb, proximity to Europe and the pull of the European Union's Neighborhood Policy and *acquis communautaire* have exerted some influence upon the PFM reform agendas in Morocco and Tunisia, as have the French budgetary reforms that have taken place since 2001.

It remains to be seen how the new generation of actionable indicators, such as PEFA, will have an impact upon the willingness of senior MENA officials to improve their PFM performance. On the positive side, it is clear that cross-economy comparative indicators such as the World Bank's *Doing Business* have played an important role in motivating senior officials in economies to undertake reforms aimed at strengthening their business environment. In Egypt, such improvements have been the source of considerable pride and have prompted progress towards reform in other areas, such as anticorruption. There is evidence that, in at least one MENA economy, PEFA indicators may have played a comparable role. However, in some respects, PFM indicators such as PEFA are qualitatively different. The *Doing Business* indicators cater to a much larger constituency, including foreign and domestic investors and business associations. They are produced annually with an explicit comparative focus. PFM reforms tend to fall in the domain of specialists. PEFA was not explicitly set up with cross-economy comparisons in mind, and the analyses are done much less frequently than once a year. For these reasons, they are unlikely to serve as a comparable motivating force for PFM reforms.

The experience of MENA economies indicates that donor engagement on PFM issues is a two-edged sword. On the positive side, the large number of economies with some type of donor supported PFM program bears witness to the considerable demand for donor resources and technical expertise on PFM issues. Beyond these economies, a number of others in the Gulf Cooperation Council (GCC) and elsewhere are purchasing technical assistance from institutions such as the World Bank and IMF on a reimbursable basis—a "market test" that provides one of the best indications of economy demand available. In addition to advice and assistance, donor engagement can be useful in "locking in" a particular reform program and generating publicity and obligations that domestic reformers can use to their advantage. Donors can also play a vital role in monitoring the implementation of various reform agendas that, as was noted above, is an area of chronic weakness in MENA. For all of these reasons, virtually no major PFM reform in MENA has been exclusively "home grown."

But donors can also pursue their own agendas in ways that can occasionally complicate a given nation's PFM reform effort. The most prominent example is West Bank and Gaza, where donors invested considerable effort and energy from 2002 to 2005 in building up the Ministry of Finance as an alternative to the President's Office for managing the PA's finances, only to change course after Hamas was elected in January 2006 and support the President's Office, and then to switch back again in July 2007 after Fatah regained control of the West Bank. Fortunately, PA institutions were durable enough to withstand such pressures. But they did take a toll.

While the situation above is unique, it is far more common to encounter problems in fostering donor coordination in aid dependent environments, which can interfere with efforts to expand budget comprehensiveness or to integrate the recurrent and capital budgets. The PA has struggled with the superficial integration of public investment expenditures into the budget. The Ministries of Planning and Finance are co-signatories to all development projects financed by donors. But in practice, they have had limited engagement in the selection of projects, as donors often elected to engage directly with line ministries, other PA institutions and local governments. As a result, projects were not considered in a framework that accounted for future recurrent costs and debt servicing capacity, and the PA budget did not adequately reflect donor financed public investment.[16] Different donors also had conflicting expectations, demands, and reporting requirements. While they called for PFM reforms since the 1990s, many donors were also under pressure to disburse to the PA and in practice and were willing to allow such reforms to take a back seat to more immediate priorities.[17]

The Substantive Lessons for Donors on PFM Reform. Chapter 2 has addressed the substantive challenges of PFM reform in MENA at length, and its findings are summarized in table 3.1. Their messages will not be repeated here. Suffice it to say that many donor-supported reforms have been too ambitious, overstating the amount of political and bureaucratic support for reform; not fully aware of the role of legacy systems and whether the necessary preconditions were in place; and in general trying to do too much within too limited a period of time and without the required capacity. At times, there is even a lack of understanding or consensus as to what reforms such as implementing a "medium term expenditure framework" or "introducing performance into the budget" will actually mean in practice. Donor programs can be far too comprehensive—seeking to solve too many problems at once—and would benefit from greater selectivity and prioritization.

There are two emerging issues that will shape donor approaches on PFM reform in the future. The first is growing use of PEFA exercises, which are likely to play a valuable role in improving the quality of donor assistance. There is considerable appetite within MENA economies for the use of PEFA assessments as a benchmarking tool, and the number of such exercises in the region is progressing steadily at a rate of two or three a year. Some GCC economies such as Kuwait are even willing to pay to have their PFM institutions and systems reviewed through the use of reimbursable technical assistance. This trend is a healthy one, in that the expanded use of PEFA will enlarge the amount of analytic work available to inform PFM reforms; help donors to better understand where the real issues and challenges are; and allow economies to monitor their performance over time, thus creating additional incentives to take PFM reforms forward. However, would be donors should also be wary in using PEFA exercises mechanistically to design reform strategies, lest they find themselves trying to "fill in the gaps." Such motives, while understandable, may well result in developing reforms for areas where a given PEFA score is low but the demand for improving it is also weak and unsustainable. PEFA is not a substitute for careful strategic analysis and decision making.

The second trend is the increasing use of political economy analysis to illuminate public sector reform options, which is covered in the first lesson of this chapter. Few would dispute that political and bureaucratic dynamics can play a decisive role in the evolution of PFM reforms, and that a careful understanding of the issues involved would be invaluable to donors interested in supporting this work. The problem, put succinctly by a leading reformer in the region, is that donors "are typically not well-equipped to do it."[18] By that, he meant that the process of PFM reform is a dynamic one requiring a great deal of insider knowledge and a lot of tactical real-time adjustments to changes in the prevailing political and bureaucratic winds. To the extent that donors will be able to capture this subtlety and nuance—whether it be through the use of embedded ministry advisors, knowledgeable local experts or some combination of both—their programs will be the better for it. However, if the exercise becomes static and routine, such as bringing in an external expert to draft a political economy report according to a standard template prior to the initiation of a major PFM reform, then much of its usefulness will be lost and the shelf life of the final product may be short.

Modalities and Processes. In a similar fashion, donor modalities need to be developed to better respond to the dynamic nature of the PFM reform process. There is a role for the traditional project management framework when the reforms are large and enduring (and the sums involved substantial), which is designed to successfully manage a broad and diverse agenda and ensure appropriate accountability. But lengthy appraisal, consultant selection and mobilization procedures often result in delays and lost opportunities. As was noted in Lesson 4 above, the more successful PMF reforms tend to involve "strategic opportunism"—seizing upon opportunities rapidly as they emerge within a broader framework of clearly articulated priorities.

To exploit such opportunities as and when they occur, donors need to augment their traditional approaches with small, rapidly disbursing, carefully targeted aid. To do this will require several preconditions: (1) accurate, up to date knowledge of the situation on the ground, including the evolving political and bureaucratic dynamics; (2) talented, advisors who have technical skills, political and managerial savvy, and the trust of senior officials; (3) a well-articulated framework of PFM priorities; and (4) small amounts of

CHAPTER 5

Algeria

David Shand
Daniel Tommasi

General Overview

Algeria is a lower-middle-income economy with a population of 33.8 million (2008 estimate). GDP per capita in 2007 is estimated at US$6,538 (PPP) and US$3,903 (nominal, IMF data). Algeria achieved independence from France in 1962 and its public financial management (PFM) and public administration systems are derived from the French administrative tradition.

Since independence, Algeria has endured considerable political turbulence, including a prolonged civil war that ended only in 1998. Lingering political instability has continued and Islamic fundamentalism remains a threat as reflected in a major upsurge in violence in 2007. While there are been a general move in recent years to open up the political process, significant restrictions remain on freedom of expression. Since 1994, Algeria has moved from central economic planning to greater liberalization of the economy, designed to improve the business climate and attract foreign investment.

Algeria has a system of strong executive government focused on the President who appoints the Prime Minister and Cabinet. Parliament is relatively weak, though growing in influence. Algeria is a multiparty state but all parties must be approved by the Ministry of the Interior. The 48 provinces (*wilayas*) play a significant role in service delivery, such as health, education, and water. Each province has its own elected assemblies and its budget. However, the governor (*wali*) who is the head of the executive of the *wilaya* has extensive powers. The *wali* is the representative of the central government. He is appointed by the President and reports to the Ministry of Interior. Each province has its own budget, for which the *wali* is the authorizing officer.

Only limited and dated PFM diagnostic information is available, including a 2005 IMF Fiscal Report on the Observance of Standards and Codes (ROSC) and a 2007 Bank Public Expenditure Review (PER). No Public Expenditure and Financial Accountability (PEFA) assessment has been undertaken or is planned.

Algeria has a clear legal and administrative framework for PFM and a reasonably functioning PFM system which provides for a satisfactory degree of financial control and external audit. Algeria has reasonable PFM staff capacity. However, the PFM system has major weaknesses in budget formulation and execution. The investment budget lacks credibility, comprehensiveness, and transparency. As discussed later, many technical weaknesses exist and antiquated procedures need to be reformed, particularly in budget execution. The main weaknesses in PFM are more institutional in nature rather than technical issues.

The 2007 PER measured Algeria's PFM practices against the 16 indicators formulated jointly by the Bank and the IMF for the heavily indebted poor economies (HIPC) exercise, on which much of the subsequent PEFA performance indicators are based. It concluded that Algeria met only 5 of the 16 benchmarks, which was below the performance of the average HIPC economy.

In 2001, Algeria embarked on an ambitious PFM modernization program supported by a US$23.7 million World Bank Loan to support a Budget System Modernization Project (BSMP) covering central government expenditures and using international consultants. There were two main components, the first comprising reforms to the budget system (including performance-based budgeting, a medium-term expenditure framework, expenditure management systems, and a strengthened expenditure control system) and the second comprising the development of an integrated budget management information system. However progress was moderately unsatisfactory, with limited government commitment during the first five years. It also appears that the inclusion of the information and communication technology (ITC) component may have led to perceptions that the project was primarily of a technical rather than an institutional nature. In 2006, the Loan was reduced in amount to US$18.4 million and extended by three years, closing in February 2009. The ITC component was limited to studies, software development, and pilots. The key player in PFM reform is the Ministry of Finance, through the Directorate of Budget Systems Modernization created in 2008.

The budget remains highly dependent on oil revenues, which represent around 80 percent of total budget revenues. Using substantially increased oil revenues in recent years, Algeria has embarked on a large public investment program known as the Complementary Plan for Support to Growth, or PCSC. This large expenditure has given rise to a need for better prioritization of investment spending. Investment expenditure is generally considered to perform poorly and there are increasing concerns that all of these funds are being used as intended. The Bank has provided assistance for the establishment of a new state agency (CNED) to better implement major infrastructure projects in the PCSC.

Since the 2000 supplementary budget law, oil revenue in excess of budget law projections is allocated to a special treasury account, the Revenue Regulation Fund (*Fond de Regulation des Recettes* or FRR), part of which has been used to make early repayments of external public debt. As a result, government debt has fallen significantly. The overall fiscal balance moved from an average deficit of 1.7 percent of GDP in 1990–95 to a surplus of 13.6 percent in 2006; 4.5 percent in 2007; and 8.1 percent in 2008. However due to the decline in oil prices, a budget deficit of around 8.4 percent of GDP is expected for 2009—the first budget deficit in a decade.

The public sector is large and expensive. It employs around 12 percent of the total workforce. The government sector wage bill comprises around one third of recurrent budget expenditures. There are significant state enterprises including the state oil company SONATRACH, the electricity and gas distribution company Sonelgaz, the Algerian Development Bank, and Algeria telecom.

Algeria lags on a number of governance indicators, although the general trend is one of improvement. In terms of World Bank Institute (WBI) Governance indicators, there have been improvements in government effectiveness, quality of administration and service delivery. However, government accountability remains weak. Corruption remains a persistent problem, reflected in Algeria's poor ranking in many major indices.

A comprehensive financial control system is in place, but focuses principally on compliance with legal procedures. The legal framework of the control and audit of the expenditures is quite clear and adequate. Internal control relies on financial controllers, government accounting officers, in-house auditors, and inspectorates of specific services. Reflecting the French system, the existing system provides for strict separation of function between those responsible for commitments and payment authorization operations (the authorizing officers, who are line ministries' officers) and those in charge of revenue collection, payment of expenses and management of funds (government accounting officers, who report to the MOF). However, monitoring is limited to financial follow-up and compliance with legal procedures. There is no performance monitoring, and the technical and physical monitoring of the investment projects made by line ministries and agencies is uneven and data are not centralized. Besides, due to the lack of skills and training of their staff, the line ministry inspectorate generals are regarded as weak.

According to the 2005 IMF ROSC, the reporting of data to parliament and to the public is largely inadequate. The Treasury produces statements on a regular basis but they are not made available to the public. No information is published on STA transactions. Moreover, the budget and financial data available are limited to central government units, even though local governments, public institutions, and social security agencies account for a significant part of public expenditure.

The Algerian system is not able to issue timely or sufficiently accurate annual public accounts. Nor are they audited in a timely manner. The draft financial settlement laws (*loi de règlement*) that present the final accounts are no longer presented to parliament.

External Scrutiny and Audit. The legal framework for external audit is comprehensive and well established. The members of the National Audit Court have the statute of magistrate and are guaranteed independence. The Court is entitled by the Constitution to oversee the finances of central government, local governments, and state enterprises. It exercises ex post controls; judges the work of all accounting officers; and investigates breaches of financial regulations. However, the 2005 IMF ROSC suggests that its professional capacity is not adequate. The Court reports to both the President and the parliament. However, its latest published annual report is for 1996–97, and its reports are not now publicly available despite an apparent requirement that they be published in full or in part in the Official Gazette.

Parliament receives the draft budget in detail as well as details of budget out-turn for the previous two years. Once passed, the budget is notified in the Official Gazette, which presents current expenditures aggregated by ministry and capital expenditures aggregated by sectors. Published data on the budget is therefore very aggregated. In addition, the financial settlement law is not presented to parliament even though audit reports are (although they are not publicly available), thus limiting parliament's follow up ability.

Implementation Strategies for Reform

The Government of Algeria's general approach has been to first approve changes in the Organic Budget law and then work on implementing the necessary technical reforms. This has led to a slow pace of actual reform.

Until 2006, the progress of the BMSP has been largely unsatisfactory. Government commitment during the initial five years of the project was uncertain. A significant number of technical tools were prepared but have not been adopted or implemented. These include a new budgetary classification, new expenditure management procedures and a computerization master plan.

The 2006 review of the Bank Loan concluded that inadequate implementation of the project was due to: (1) frequent changes in project management leading to poor oversight; (2) highly ambitious and poorly defined project objectives; and (3) lack of interagency coordination, including a failure by MOF to adequately engage line ministries. As a result, the Government and the Bank thoroughly reviewed the program and agreed to scale it back and break the process down into smaller building blocks. Project implementation started to become effective in 2006–07 mainly because of changes in project management.

As a result, progress has been made since 2007–08. A new organization chart for the MOF was established in November 2007. The separate Recurrent and Capital Budget units have been merged. The pilot program budgeting carried out during FY07 has been not been pursued during FY08 for unknown reasons, but it should resume in FY09. More importantly, a draft Organic Budget Law was approved in 2008 by the Council of Government (which includes all ministers and is chaired by the Prime Minister), although it has not yet been approved by the Council of Ministers, which is chaired by the President, notably because of the Presidential elections. Except for a few provisions, this new Law provides an adequate legal framework for implementing program budgeting.

A strategy for PFM reform was drafted by consultants in 2007, and its proposals are incorporated in the draft Organic Budget Law. The general approach has been a comprehensive one, with pilots used only in program budgeting. As a general rule, small, discrete reforms have not been attempted. There are difficulties in carrying out pilots or selective reforms in Algeria because of its administrative culture—which tends to favor a top-down tradition in undertaking reform based on laws and regulations rather than those that involve studies and pilots. Nevertheless the pilots have fed into the provisions of the draft Organic Budget Law and the current program budgeting work.

Other relevant factors include the central role of the MOF and a general risk aversion towards initiatives not sanctioned from the highest level. No specific incentives have been provided to individuals or organizations to promote or accept the reforms.

The scope of the reform is potentially broad. The February 2009 final supervision mission for the BSMP Loan indicated that important elements for future reform are ready for adoption. The new Organic Budget Law already approved by the Council of Government sets out the reform direction. It includes a new program classification, multiyear budgeting, performance monitoring, the definition of the content of the budget documents, a new chart of accounts and partial accrual based accounting (but not budgeting). Various studies on budget execution procedures have been prepared by the consultants, but no decision on changes has been made. There may be a concern that relaxing inputs controls would be seen as encouraging corruption.

A directorate within the MOF is in charge of the reform program, but the arrangements to supervise the preparation of the new FMIS are unclear. The BSMP coordinator (recently appointed as director of the new Budget Reform Directorate in MOF) has been the de facto manager in charge of implementation. Planning and implementation of BSMP activities has been based on the Bank project and more or less followed, although with significant delays.

There have been no overall reform strategies in line ministries. Real ownership of the multiyear approach and performance budgeting pilots by the line ministries is uncertain. Likewise ownership by the *wali* is also questionable. However, the draft Organic Budget Law was extensively discussed with line ministries before finalization.

Political Economy of Reform

The complex nature of Algerian society means there are many conflicting forces in public sector reform. Within the bureaucracy, there are differences between MOF technical staff who are interested in recent European (and particularly French reforms), and the *wali* or governors who wish to retain their traditional power and influence over expenditure. Other prominent players include the line ministries, powerful state enterprises who are keen to preserve their autonomy and the army. A further division occurs in society between the westernized and the traditional point of view, which at its highest level is reflected in the views of whoever is the Prime Minister at any point in time. All this makes reform difficult and complex. In addition, Algeria has not shown interest in demonstrating to external parties such as the EC and the financial markets that it attaches priority to PFM reforms. This likely reflects its healthy oil revenues and the expectation that they will continue.

Overall, the broader political environment has hindered reforms. Other political priorities after the war with terrorism and a general lack of political and technical commitment explain the lack of progress from 2001 to 2005. There was no director of the Budget General Directorate in place for several years, only an acting director. The appointment of a new Minister of Finance and then a new Prime Minister in 2006–07, who had some interest in and support for the reforms, has been important in the improved progress since then. The heads of the General Budget Department and the Public Accounting Department have also been supporting the reforms.

In 2007, the main opposition to the reforms came from the governors, who feared that the program-budget approach would reinforce the role of sector ministries and diminish their financial powers. This issue is quite important in Algeria, given the high degree of de-concentration and the power of governors. As a result, the Ministry of the Interior and governors tried to slow down the reforms. A meeting was held at the highest political level to resolve this issue, and the draft Organic Budget law reflects a compromise. It stipulates that a part of the commitment appropriation may be allotted to governors. However, it appears that this conflict has not yet been fully resolved, which may delay the approval of the draft Organic Budget Law.

Within line ministries, some think that the reforms will not bring any enduring change. Some see an opportunity to regain control over the sector policy, which tends currently to be defined by other players such as the governors. Others may perceive increased transparency or streamlining of budget execution controls as a threat to their private interests.

As mentioned earlier, the reform is focusing on policy based budgeting, as provided for in the new Organic Budget law, rather than the more difficult area of streamlining budget execution.

The economy is not aid dependent and donors have very little influence on government decision making. While government technocrats may need external expertise to modernize the PFM system, they are more influenced by the need to comply with the prevailing political priorities. At the political level, Algeria clearly prefers to handle PFM reforms in its own way without involvement of donors.

Algeria's membership of peer organizations has not been a significant factor influencing its reforms. Comparisons with Sub-Saharan Africa economies may be counterproductive, but there appears to be interest in comparisons with the other Maghreb economies. The French budgetary reform and discussions on the Canadian budget system with the consultants have encouraged reformers within the MOF and some line ministries.

Key Conclusions

Increased transparency and better budgeting process are needed but, as noted, these are not mere technical issues. Therefore, the question is whether the reform measures will be able to make the institutional processes more transparent and to improve policy decision making.

An important lesson is related to the period 2001–05. Launching a PFM project needs clear government ownership and agreement on the objectives of reforms. Including a significant IT component may help to facilitate agreement on the project, but the project may, in turn, be seen as a primarily technical exercise rather than one which seeks to change the way policy decisions on revenues and expenditures are made. In an economy like Algeria, project implementation is unlikely to be successful if the project objectives are not appropriately defined.

formation of a MENA regional group of senior budget officials that is modeled on the OECD arrangement and follows the example set by several other regions of the world. Egypt hosted the first meeting of the regional group in Cairo in November 2009. Economies of the region will come together periodically to learn about each other's experiences and discuss topical PFM issues of importance to budget officials. It is too early to say what the added value of these meetings will be, but if OECD experience is anything to go by, they have the potential to strengthen regional collaboration and support valuable PFM reform lesson-learning.

Key Conclusions

Egypt's experience during the past decade clearly illustrates that successful implementation of PFM reform is much more than a technical exercise. With the support of donors, and under the leadership of the Ministry of Finance, Egypt has tackled many of the crucial dimensions of PFM. Progress has undoubtedly been made—particularly in the area of tax and customs reform—where the lessons from Egypt's experience will no doubt be valuable to other economies embarking upon similar reforms. Yet it has not been uniform. Looking forward, the Government may wish to give attention to several areas:

- developing an overarching strategic framework, within which reforms can be planned, prioritized, sequenced, costed, evaluated for feasibility, and monitored
- ensuring that Egypt's PFM capacity is not stretched too thinly to cope effectively with the myriad reform initiatives that have been initiated
- making sure that adequate resources are allocated to implement reforms
- ensuring that project managers are appointed with appropriate delegated authority
- thinking more carefully about developing effective change management processes and skills, and communicating the case for and benefits of reform to promote real understanding and ownership.

Notes

1. See www.openbudgetindex.org.
2. It is understood that a PFM reform strategy has now been drafted and is currently under consideration by the Ministry of Finance.
3. The Minister of Finance, recognizing the need for a more systematic approach to capacity development, has recently decided that a Ministry of Finance training center be established as a vehicle for more effective training planning and implementation.
4. World Bank, *Egypt Country Financial Accountability Assessment, 2008.*
5. As long ago as 2005/06, the budget circular referred to "jump-starting" the decentralization policy and maximizing the role of localities.
6. It is understood that the Government of Egypt has already decided to establish a modern internal audit system but this reform appears to be delayed while plans for institutional reform of the MOF are being finalized.
7. This practice is found in many parts of the Egyptian civil service.

CHAPTER 7

Iraq

David F. Biggs

General Overview

Iraq is composed of eighteen administrative divisions, known as governorates, three of which comprise the Kurdistan Regional Government (KRG). It is governed in terms of its October 2005 Constitution, which commits Iraq to become a federal state. The executive branch of Government comprises a Head of State; President Jalal Talabani (since April 2005); and a Head of Government, Prime Minister Nuri al-Maliki (since May 2006). The legislative branch consists of a unicameral Council of Representatives or *Mejlis Watani* (consisting of 275 members elected by a closed-list, proportional-representation system). The judicial branch and legal system include a Supreme Court appointed by the Prime Minister, confirmed by the Presidency Council.

The past six years have been dominated by the overthrow of the Saddam Hussein regime and its replacement with a fledgling democracy. Security has been a major concern, inhibiting the efforts by the Government of Iraq (GoI) and its international partners to modernize Iraqi social, economic, and political life. Nevertheless, the GoI has engaged with the international community and produced an International Compact which acts as a kind of partnership agreement between Iraq and its international supporters. Prominent in the Compact is the need to improve governance, including public financial management (PFM). The latter is particularly important in the context of Iraq given its huge oil reserves and revenues that place a premium on the efficient and effective management of public resources.

A major feature of the PFM reform process since 2003 has been the considerable emphasis placed on budget execution, where there have been major problems in the implementation of capital projects. New control and accountability organizations, notably the Commission of Integrity (COI) and the Inspectors General, have been created. Like more established organizations, they have major capacity development challenges.

Support for PFM has been forthcoming from a range of multilateral and bilateral sources, including the United States, the United Kingdom, the European Commission (EC), the International Monetary Fund (IMF), and the World Bank. By far the largest individual donor has been the United States, which has invested heavily in improving PFM. Various parts of the U.S. Government, including the Treasury, State Department, and United States Agency for International Development (USAID) have financed accounting reform, budget formulation and implementation, the introduction of a financial management information system, and the strengthening of accountability and financial control. In a number of these areas, the United States has worked alongside the United Kingdom's Department for International Development (DFID). Both the IMF and the World Bank have provided technical assistance and support for capacity development. The EC has financed a US$20 million PFM reform project under the aegis of the World Bank administered Iraq Trust Fund (ITF) that became active in 2009.

Substantive Reform Agenda

In partnership with the Government of Iraq, the World Bank completed a Public Expenditure and Financial Accountability (PEFA) assessment in 2008 as part of its Public Expenditure and Institutional Assessment (PEIA). A summary of the performance indicator scores is in the annex to this chapter. A summary of the analysis is provided below.

Budget Credibility. Overall, the originally approved GoI budget is a rather unreliable instrument of government policy. In all three years reviewed, the variance between actual expenditure and budgeted expenditure exceeded 15 percent of budgeted expenditure. Revenues have been consistently exceeding budgeted amounts by a significant margin, whereas actual expenditure—particularly in regard to capital investments—has consistently been well below budget. The inevitable consequence was large budget surpluses in 2006 and 2007, leading to a big increase in the stock of cash reserves in the Development Fund for Iraq held in New York. In addition, better monitoring of expenditure payment arrears is required.

Comprehensiveness and Transparency. The PEFA assessment examines which of nine pieces of "good practice" information are included in the budget documentation submitted to the Parliament. In Iraq, four of these were found to be included in the GoI budget papers, but they tended to be partial rather than complete (for example, key budget tables are frequently missing). These four elements are: (1) key macroeconomic assumptions; (2) fiscal balance; (3) consistent reporting of current and budget year; and (4) summarized data for revenue and expenditure. There is a significant level of unreported government operations and weak oversight of fiscal risk arising from the activities of other public sector entities. A particular problem relates to donor activities that are generally not covered in the budget. GFS-based economic classifications are now being used during budget formulation in addition to primary administrative classifications. While a functional classification was absent at the time of the assessment, it is being developed, and is included at an aggregate level in the 2010 budget.

Policy-Based Budgeting. Although the budgetary process is fairly orderly, there is room for improvement in a number of areas. These include improving the budget strategy and the Budget Call Circular; introducing the use of budget ceilings that reflect government policy priorities and avoid work on the production of unrealistically high budget submissions by ministries and other government agencies; strengthening the coordination of the recurrent and capital components of the budget; and the development of a multiyear perspective in financial planning and budgeting.

Predictability and Control in Budget Execution. This dimension covers a wide range of PFM issues, including tax administration, budget releases, cash and debt management, procurement, internal financial and payroll controls, and internal audit. With the exception of tax collection, tax administration was relatively sound. But payroll controls were found to be weak, and internal controls (including internal audit) were of limited effectiveness. Procurement procedures are non-transparent and lack competition. In an environment of extensive reconstruction, this is one of the factors contributing to allegations of corruption in Iraq.

Accounting, Recording, and Reporting. This was generally a weak area with no available information on the resources received by service delivery units are and deficiencies in the quality and timeliness of annual financial statements. There was a need to document the Iraqi government accounting framework so as to create greater certainty and understanding of the legal and regulatory requirements on the part of finance and accounting staff.[1] There were problems with the quality and timeliness of both in-year budget reports and annual financial statements. Both were hampered by the lack of a functioning financial management information system.

External Scrutiny and Audit. Weaknesses exist in terms of timely submission of audit reports to the Council of Representatives and follow-up on audit recommendations. Parliamentary scrutiny of the budget needs to be strengthened by the establishment of a well-resourced budget office.

Donor Assistance. The performance of the Iraqi PFM system has not been helped by the operations of donors, who do not score well against the PEFA indicators. The financial information they provide is untimely, incomplete, and not delivered in line with the GoI's budget cycle or in a breakdown consistent with the Government's classification system. In addition, national procedures are bypassed for almost all development assistance projects and programs.

Summary of Substantive Reforms. The impact of these PFM weaknesses may be assessed against the three standard objectives of PFM systems: macro-fiscal discipline, strategic allocation of resources, and operational or technical efficiency. These three objectives are linked. Fiscal discipline is the basis without which neither a strategic allocation of resources nor operational efficiency is possible.

For a few years, high world oil prices enabled the GoI to generate much higher revenues than budgeted. Consequently, during that period which ended in the second half of 2008, the GoI experienced no difficulty in financing a growing level of public expenditure. On the contrary, it was able to accumulate significant reserves of foreign currency through its budget surpluses. While oil prices remained buoyant, maintaining macro-fiscal discipline posed few problems, but now the situation has changed dramatically. Even before the collapse of oil prices, measures needed to be taken to contain recurrent expenditure and achieve a higher level of capital investment budget execution.

Strategic resource allocations in Iraq suffer from the lack of a medium term perspective to budgeting and financial planning. Although a strategic medium term fiscal perspective exists in conjunction with the International Compact for Iraq (ICI), it is difficult to see the connection between this and annual resource allocations. Budgeting continues to be primarily an annual exercise. The problem is compounded by the lack of effective integration between the recurrent and investment budgets both at the aggregate level and at the sectoral level.

A major issue in Iraq over the last few years has been the low budget execution rate for capital investment, which has prevented the effective development of essential public services. The difficult security situation has clearly been an important factor, but there are also systemic PFM issues associated with budget formulation and implementation. While at times there have been problems with the release of allocations that have limited the accessibility of budget funds to ministries and governorates, there is also a major issue in terms of the inefficient use of funds that have been released but have remained idle in the bank accounts of spending units.

PFM Reform Priorities. Having spent many years largely isolated from the international community, Iraq's PFM system inevitably has required and continues to require reform and modernization across all its major dimensions. Since 2003, support for a demanding reform agenda has been forthcoming from a number of external parties, but progress has generally been slow and difficult due to a range of factors that include the difficult security situation, the loss of significant numbers of experienced and qualified staff leading to low capacity in the system, inadequate reform program design, and the absence of a coherent reform strategy and action plan that all Iraq's development partners can support.

Much donor support has been devoted to improving Iraq's budgeting practice, especially with a view to raising capital budget execution rates. The United States has been particularly keen to see the GoI making better use of its own budgeted resources as well as those provided in aid. Since 2003, Iraq has made some progress in reforming public expenditure management. This appears to have had a positive impact on capital budget execution rates, which are reported to have risen from 49 percent in 2005 to 60 percent in 2007. However, there are still many issues that need to be addressed if capital budget performance is to be optimized. The PEIA identified a range of bottlenecks in the capital investment budgeting system, stretching from procurement and contract management through commitment, verification, and payment to oversight. Wide divergences had also been observed in budget execution rates between ministries and between governorates. Only the relatively stable and more secure region of Kurdistan had been able to achieve a high level of budget implementation.

Budget preparation reform is also a priority. Among the improvements necessary are:

- a better process and content for Iraq's budget strategy
- a revised Budget Call Circular (BCC) that includes priority-based, sectoral budget ceilings in order to facilitate the submission of realistic budget proposals by government departments and agencies
- better integration of the recurrent and capital components of the budget formulation processes, including institutional reform measures
- development of a medium-term perspective as a framework for the annual budgeting exercise
- introducing a functional classification of the budget as a step towards the eventual use of a program classification
- expanding the scope of the information contained in the budget papers to improve transparency and accountability
- incorporating donor-financed activities in the national budget
- closer adherence to the BCC.

Some progress has been made in modernizing government accounting and reporting, but the work is far from complete. A new GFS-compliant economic classification system and complementary chart of accounts have been developed and introduced, but implementation remains a work-in-progress and requires a considerable amount of training and capacity development. The legal requirements for government accounting are poorly understood with considerable confusion in the minds of government finance staff over the respective status of the Financial Management Law introduced by the Coalition Provisional Authority in 2005 and previously extant legislation. In order to clarify the situation, a working group was established by the GoI charged with the responsibility of documenting the government accounting framework. With the support of the U.S. and the U.K. Governments, as well as the World Bank, this exercise has been more or less completed with the drafting of a comprehensive accounting user manual that can as a source of reference for accounting practitioners.

One of the main obstacles to improved financial reporting continues to be the absence of a properly functioning government financial management information system (FMIS). Despite the fact that the development and implementation of such a system was the subject of heavy investment by the United States, progress has been mixed. The program was close to being abandoned when in 2008 a Memorandum of Understanding was signed between the United States and the GoI to restart the program. USAID hired BearingPoint to relaunch the IFMIS project (see box 7.1).

Box 7.1. The Iraq Financial Information Management System

Recognizing the importance of an automated financial reporting system, the GoI attempted, with the support of the U.S. Government, to develop and implement the Iraq Financial Management Information System (IFMIS). USAID-contracted consultants who worked with GoI counterparts to develop and implement the system using a Free Balance Financials software package, and hardware was centralized within the MOF in Baghdad. The IFMIS was an automated accounting system intended initially to improve budget execution. Other modules were to be added as part of a gradual move towards a more complete financial management information system. Several reviews of the system were conducted, including those undertaken by the IMF/World Bank in 2005 and that of the U.S. Government's Special Inspector General for Iraqi Reconstruction (SIGIR) in 2007.

The joint Bank/IMF mission in 2005 reported problems with the project that needed to be addressed in the next few months notwithstanding the difficult conditions under which both the consultants and GoI officials were working. Most notable perhaps was the absence of a conceptual design document, which international experience shows to be a key requirement if project risk is to be contained. This would have helped define the high-level functional requirements with participation from major stakeholders, like the accounting and other key directorates in the MOF, including the budget department and the Ministry of Planning and Development Cooperation (MOPDC), as well as major line agencies. It would have also assisted in deciding on the workable systems architecture and hardware and communication requirements and training needs leading to a relevant IT strategy for the project implementation. Crucially, it would have increased understanding and ownership of the project on the part of system users.

The PEIA workshop in 2007 elicited from participating GoI officials the assessment that more work was needed to establish the preconditions necessary for reform. The Bank's analysis identified the following six main obstacles:

- unsatisfactory project supervision and contract management arrangements
- lack of support for and recognition of Project Management Teams
- insufficient or inappropriate incentives to promote the Government's PFM reform agenda
- inadequate consultative, coordination and co-financing arrangements to support high levels of ownership, effective partnerships and high degrees of commitment from key stakeholders

(Box continues on next page)

Implementation and sustainability of reforms in the past six years or so have been undermined by the very difficult security environment and the acute capacity shortages in the PFM system. The latter challenge has not been helped by the creation of new institutions like the Inspectors General and the Commission of Integrity (COI) that have been grafted onto the existing system. Even long-established organizations like the BSA are in need of modernization and greater contact with the international community. In these circumstances, it is difficult—and perhaps unrealistic—to point to any single outstanding example of a successful PFM reform. Instead, a range of initiatives have been undertaken, all of which have made some progress, though typically less than was hoped for. On the downside, the FMIS reform has probably been one of the most disappointing, while recognizing that the introduction of a nationwide system during a period of conflict was a tall order.

It may well be the case that reform has been tackled on too many fronts at once given the conditions on the ground in Iraq. Until recently, there was no government-owned PFM reform strategy and action plan, so initiatives have tended to be piecemeal and lacking coherence. An overriding need in Iraq is to restore and enhance the capacity of the Iraqi PFM system. The events of the past six years have witnessed devastating losses to institutions, organizations, and human capital. Many experienced staff have been lost to the public service at the same time as new institutional arrangements and organizations have been created or replaced. Physical infrastructure has been destroyed and the effective functioning of the PFM system has been severely undermined by the difficult security environment. It will take a sustained and comprehensive capacity development program fully supported by the international development community to help Iraq to overcome these problems.

An integrated PFM reform program is clearly necessary. This needs to be led by the GoI and supported over the medium term by Iraq's international development partners. Careful consideration should be given to ensuring a sustainable pace of reform that does not exceed the absorptive capacity of the Iraqi PFM system. International experience demonstrates the importance of properly sequenced and resourced PFM reform programs backed by political and administrative champions. It also shows the value of adopting a "building blocks" or "platform approach" to PFM reform. This minimizes the risk of embarking on the reform of PFM components before the time is right. Essentially, the underlying philosophy is one of getting the basics right before tackling more sophisticated and challenging issues.

Implementation Strategies for Reform

At a strategic level, the importance of PFM reform has been recognized and acknowledged. PFM issues occupy a prominent place in the International Compact for Iraq (ICI), which is a framework for cooperation with the international community. Benchmarks and milestones have been set in the accompanying monitoring matrix, though in practice delays have typically occurred in the implementation of reforms. But the management of the PFM reform process in Iraq has suffered from the absence of any overall vision, strategy, or prioritized and logically sequenced action plan. Reforms have been tackled in an opportunistic manner, often prompted by the advice or requirements of Iraq's international partners.

The PFM reform process is led by the Ministry of Finance. Other key stakeholders are the Ministry of Planning (in relation to the capital investment budget); the Office of the Prime Minister (OPM); the office of the Deputy Prime Minister (ODPM); the BSA (in relation to the external audit of the public sector and accounting standards); the Inspectors General (internal audit and investigations in government departments); and the COI (investigations into allegations of fraud and corruption). The Council of Representatives (the Iraqi Parliament) is also seeking to strengthen its contribution to effective PFM through enhanced budget scrutiny, facilitated by a proposed budget office. Iraq's constitutional commitment to a federal state has led in the last two or three annual budgets to far greater decentralization of public spending to subnational government in the form of the governorates and the Kurdistan Regional Government (KRG). Outstanding issues in the KRG concern the completion of merging two administrations, including the Ministry of Finance and Board of Supreme Audit.

Problems have arisen during the implementation of individual reform programs as a result of limited authority and resources being delegated to program managers. Too often, decisions have to be referred up the hierarchy in a way that stifles initiative and provides little incentive to the managers and undermines ownership of and commitment to the reform process.

Incentives in general appear to be a problematic area in the Iraqi civil service. Prior to the overthrow of the Saddam regime in 2003, a staff incentives scheme existed, but this was suspended by the Coalition Provisional Authority (CPA). In addition, staff motivation is undermined by the absence of a performance evaluation system based on objective criteria that would recognize and reward good performance. Politicization of ministries is commonplace, with political and tribal allegiance and loyalty being the primary basis for recruitment and promotion.

Political Economy of Reform

From a general political standpoint, the period under review has been one of great instability characterized by volatile governance arrangements. Iraq has seen a governing authority established by an occupying power, a transitional national government, and a more permanent government that came to power through a newly established democratic process that was boycotted by many disillusioned voters. Similar skepticism prevailed during the first provincial elections, but the second set of provincial elections attracted much wider participation and greater acceptance. At the national level, boycotts of both government and parliament by sectarian political parties have occurred on a fairly regular basis. Parliament lacked a speaker for a protracted period of time. Thus the environment for public sector reform has been extremely challenging, especially as various ministries have been "captured" and ministerial posts have been shared out among the leading political groups.

The post-2003 period has witnessed attempts to promote considerable change that often represents a major departure from traditional norms and practice. New organizations have been created and significant amendments have been made to the legal and regulatory framework, often without much regard to the pre-existing laws and often failing to secure the required full understanding and acceptance of those public officials responsible for managing public finances. A great deal of uncertainty has arisen regard-

CHAPTER 8

Jordan

David F. Biggs

General Overview

Jordan is a constitutional monarchy divided into 12 administrative divisions, or governorates. Legislation is rooted in its 1952 Constitution as amended. The executive branch of government is led by a Head of State, King Abdullah II (since February 1999) and the Prime Minister as the Head of Government. The legislative branch has a bicameral National Assembly or *Majlis al-'Umma*. It consists of the Senate, also called the House of Notables or *Majlis al-Ayan* in Arabic (which has 55 seats with its members appointed by the monarch for four-year terms); and the House of Representatives, also called the House of Deputies or *Majlis al-Nuwaab* (which has 110 seats, with its members elected by popular vote on the basis of proportional representation to serve four-year terms). The electoral system has been subject to frequent reform, and in the wake of the political protests in the region during 2011, further changes are being proposed to the method of representation and how individual representatives are elected. Jordanian law is based on civil law and Islamic legal principles. The court system is divided into religious, civil, and special courts. At the apex of the judicial hierarchy is the Court of Cassation, or the Supreme Court of Appeal.

On most aspects of governance, Jordan continues to be a high performer in both the region and among economies at a similar level of development. According to a number of global governance indicators, Jordan performs well on control of corruption, government effectiveness, regulatory quality, and rule of law, with the control of corruption being its highest score. The economy's 2007 score on internal bank rankings was above the Middle East and North Africa (MENA) region average and close to the scores of the Gulf States. Jordan and the Gulf states also top Transparency International's chart for the region. The Global Integrity Index for 2008 gave Jordan a rank of "moderate"—the highest ranking of any MENA economy, with particularly high marks for access to justice, anticorruption agency and law enforcement, government effectiveness, rule of law and regulatory quality.

Despite Jordan's generally impressive performance, challenges remain. While Jordan may have quite solid performance in terms of international comparators, popular expectations are rising and the public appears more critical of the Government's performance. According to the WGI, the level of political stability in Jordan, while not as critical as in conflict ravaged Iraq or West Bank and Gaza, is below MENA average and below the mean for lower-middle income economies. This problem is linked in turn to frequent government changes and cabinet reshuffles that impede the Government's ability to undertake meaningful structural reforms.

Jordan's public financial management (PFM) reform efforts have attracted significant donor support from both multilateral and bilateral sources. The International Monetary Fund (IMF) is involved in supporting a macro-fiscal unit, as well as on treasury and cash management issues. The World Bank has been supporting a variety of public sector reform initiatives, ranging from a joint expenditure review with the government to assistance developing capacities for macro-fiscal modeling in the MOF. More recently, Bank assistance has focused on support for the introduction of a Medium Term Expenditure Framework (MTEF) and policy driven budget process.

Among bilateral donors, the United States Agency for International Development (USAID) is the most heavily involved in PFM reform through a US$40 million project that has PFM as is its main component. The main areas of USAID focus are budget reforms—including results oriented budgeting—and implementing a Government Financial Management Information System (GFMIS). The German development agency GTZ has had a long-term involvement in the PFM reform area in Jordan, focusing particularly on budget issues, although in future they intend to focus on internal control issues in cooperation with the European Union (EU). The EU provides budget support for PFM reform to support sustainable economic growth and fiscal consolidation, as well as various sectoral reforms.

Substantive Reform Agenda

There are two relatively recent assessments of Jordan's PFM performance. A Public Expenditure and Financial Accountability (PEFA) assessment, sponsored by the European Union, took place during the spring of 2007. It concluded that "Jordan has made big progress in public finance management during the last years in terms of planning, controlling, monitoring and securing greater transparency of its fiscal policies, budget implementation and debt management."[1] In August 2009, a joint IMF/World Bank review titled, *Jordan: Advancing the PFM Reform Agenda*, concluded that, "the authorities have made considerable progress in advancing PFM reforms, actively supported by donors."[2] The reviews confirm that PFM has been high on the reform agenda of both the Government of Jordan and its international development partners, and that positive results have been achieved.

A summary of the performance PEFA indicator scores is in the annex to this chapter. Using a four-point rating scale, the assessment produces the results shown in table 8.1. The table reveals a good set of results, with 19 out of 28 (68 percent) of the performance

Table 8.1. Summary of Jordan's PEFA Indicator Scores

PEFA Score	Number of Indicators
A (best)	6
B	13
C	7
D (worst)	5[a]
Total	31[b]

Source: World Bank.
Note: a. Includes 2 of the 3 donor indicators that form part of the PEFA framework.
b. Comprises 28 system indicators and 3 donor indicators.

indicators being scored as B or better. In the PEFA framework, the 28 indicators are divided into six dimensions of PFM, which are discussed below. A full presentation of the PEFA indicators for Jordan is provided in the annex to this chapter.

Budget Credibility. The PEFA assessment showed mixed results for the four indicators that refer to budget credibility. While the rating for aggregate expenditure and revenue budget variances were modest, there were problems with expenditure composition and payment arrears. The PEFA assessment attributed these to two factors, one specific (namely increases in oil price subsidies and in aid to Iraqi refugees), and the other generic (the lack of an accounting system based on commitments resulting in the absence of a system to monitor arrears). The assessment asserted that the waiving of oil price subsidies and the introduction in 2007 of a new system of accounting and monitoring taking into consideration commitments would allow Jordan in the future to improve substantially the two low scores (D). However, the 2009 Fund/Bank review noted the continuing need to develop some basic PFM systems, such as commitment controls, to address the challenge of fiscal consolidation and the risk of accumulation of expenditure arrears in particular. This was seen as one of the factors that had prevented Jordan's public finances from benefitting fully from the introduction of more advanced budgeting approaches in terms of budget credibility and aggregate fiscal discipline. In essence, one of the basics of a well performing PFM system was not fully in place.

Comprehensiveness and Transparency. Jordan scored very well in terms of the six PEFA performance indicators related to comprehensiveness and transparency. Budget formulation and execution are based on administrative, economic, and subfunctional classifications, using GFS/COFOG standards. Recent budget documentation was found to fulfill seven of the nine information benchmarks required by transparent practice, with one omission being a list of financial assets and the other the medium-term budget framework which is now provided. Prominent among the successes identified by the Fund/Bank review was the adoption of a new GFSM 2001-compliant budget classification and Chart of Accounts.

Policy-Based Budgeting. The PEFA made a positive assessment of policy-based budgeting. The budget process was considered to be regular and orderly with a clear calendar—although it would be improved if the budget was approved by the Parliament before the end of the fiscal year. Among the important reforms in this area have been initial steps on establishing a MTEF and introducing a results focus to the budget.

During the last three years, steady progress had been made in reforming the process of budget preparation as part of the MTEF reform. However, the Fund/Bank report indicated that the Minister of Finance was concerned that the reform had not yet resulted in significant improvements in public resource utilization. The analysis of the report indicated that the design of the reform was basically sound but pointed to two underlying problems: (1) the limited attention given to expenditure analysis within the government, and particularly within the General Budget Directorate (GBD); and (2) the tendency to treat current expenditure as "non-discretionary" and exempt from serious scrutiny.

The review emphasized the importance of focusing more on improved implementation rather than further consideration of the design of the reform. It also advised the implementation of a number of measures in the context of the 2011 budget cycle, including:

- GBD to introduce a revised calendar for the 2011 Budget that: (i) sets out the key stages and deadlines; (ii) provides more time for expenditure review and strategy analysis; and (iii) makes specific requirements for consultation with Cabinet at key stages during budget preparation.

- MOF/GBD to prepare a budget policy and priorities paper for discussion in Cabinet at the outset of budget preparation.
- MOF/GBD to prepare a budget framework paper for discussion and approval by Cabinet prior to issuing the Budget Circular and resource ceilings.
- Changes to the forward estimates (FEs) exercise should be introduced with the 2011 Budget to broaden its focus from prioritizing new capital spending projects towards wider program level reform initiatives.
- A "planning reserve" should be introduced into the forward estimates to provide space in the outer years of the MTEF to accommodate new spending initiatives that have not yet been identified or appraised.

While the focus on improved implementation of the reform is undoubtedly important, a separate World Bank review of the MTEF process in 2009 had some interesting insights on the reasons for weak implementation.[3] The review noted that the MTEF in Jordan had been initiated at a time when the MOF and GBD had been heavily involved in the implementation of other public finance management initiatives, such as the GF-MIS and the new chart of accounts. These other reforms have significantly limited the time and capacities available to focus on the MTEF (see box 8.1).

Box 8.1. Definition and Scope of the MTEF

The term Medium Term Expenditure Framework (MTEF) is defined to be a comprehensive budget planning process. Specifically, it includes the following stages: (1) the development of the macro-fiscal framework that determines the overall availability of resources; (2) overall budget policy and strategy analysis; (3) review of sectoral/ministry strategies and expenditure programs; (4) setting and approval of budget resource ceilings; (5) preparation of the detailed budget for the coming year and Forward Estimates (FEs) for the following two years; and (6) review and approval of the draft Budget by Cabinet and the Parliament.

The focus of the MTEF reforms is on stages (1) to (4), which together constitute the strategic phase to budget development. The MTEF reforms in Jordan have emphasized a results-oriented budgeting (ROB) approach involving the introduction of performance indicators and the feedback of performance monitoring information into the subsequent rolling forward of the MTEF. The ROB approach cuts across a number of the stages in MTEF development.[4]

Source: MOF website.

The second major reform aimed at improving the policy focus of the budget is the introduction of a performance focus through "results oriented budgeting" (ROB). This has been on the reform agenda in Jordan for more than a decade, although during most of this period progress was limited. A performance budgeting initiative was first assisted by GTZ Germany from 1999 to 2004, but it had little impact and was regarded as being too ambitious. From 2004, an ROB approach continued to be discussed and pilots were initiated in various ministries, but there appeared to be little ownership of this initiative by the GBD. The 2009 Fund/Bank report commented on the latest phase of this reform that started in 2008 with support from USAID. The report commented that impressive progress had been made in a short time, although much remained to be done. The report's recommendations covered various aspects of the new ROB approach, including

recommendations provided, and there had been insufficient guidance on the prioritiza-tion and sequencing of reform and on managing institutional and capacity constraints.

The critical conditions for success of the reforms were directly related to removing some of the obstacles associated with previous reform efforts, and included: (1) strong leadership by the Cabinet, Minister of Finance and project managers in the MOF; (2) a clear link between budget reform and the government's main policy priorities: (3) effec-tive coordination between the central ministries, line ministries, and de-concentrated lev-els of government; (4) strong integration of budget reform and the overall public sector reform effort, in particular to enhance capacity for reform management; and (5) careful sequencing of the reform effort to ensure its full realism given the capacity constraints.

The reviews have also emphasized the importance of firmly anchoring budget re-form efforts in the line management of the MOF and the GBD, which has been more effective than the establishment of special project teams and groups with separate staff to implement reforms. The latter approach has a tendency to distance these units from the day-to-day operations of the organizations concerned, as well as to make it difficult to fully integrate the new practices. It has been suggested that attempts to implement reforms through projects might also give wrong signals about the time and resource inputs required to achieve real change.

The 2004 review commented that the interagency task forces established by the MOF to implement the TSA and the MTFF appeared to be working well and might be replicated in the budget area. These task forces could serve as counterparts to advi-sors and consultants provided by international organizations and bilateral technical as-sistance (TA) providers. Finally, it made the point that fundamental reforms in budget preparation must have strong leadership within the government, and that most of the work in developing the new mechanisms must be carried out within the ministries and departments themselves. It was not possible to establish any well-functioning system such as a GFMIS or an MTEF mainly through the use of foreign consultants and advi-sors. Consultants and advisors could be very effective when used selectively, in areas that are clearly defined by the authorities themselves. But they should always play a supporting rather than leading role.

Political Economy of Reform

There are a number of political and institutional factors that have hampered PFM reform in Jordan. In particular, Jordan has a history of frequent changes of ministers. This has added a degree of high-level volatility and uncertainty to government reform initiatives that has impacted adversely on the PFM reform process. Further, as mentioned above, the institutional fragmentation of various PFM functions between the MOF, MOP, and GBD has been suboptimal and made it more difficult to establish a cohesive reform agen-da. Finally, as recognized by the 2009 Fund/Bank review, it is not clear that there has been wide ownership of the reform process beyond the central ministries and agencies.

The 2009 Fund/Bank review also identifies fiscal stress as a factor that could impinge on progress in the short term. In particular, the drive towards PFM reform in Jordan fac-es the risk of receiving less attention from senior management within the MOF because of the fiscal impact of the financial and economic crisis. The MOF is currently embarking on a series of ambitious and costly reform projects which necessitate strong support and commitment from the highest levels of the ministry in order to stay on track. GFMIS, for instance, is drawing intensively on the ministry's resources and is a high return/high risk type of project that can only succeed with strong political and managerial support. At the same time, the MOF is facing the challenge of fiscal consolidation. There is some risk that the short term pressures on Jordan's fiscal balance might force medium-term structural reforms on the back burner.

Looking over the past decade, it is possible to discern other political economy issues impacting on the PFM reform process. One example concerns a major reform of the income tax regime attempted in mid-2006 with significant TA input from USAID, which resulted in the submission of a package of reforms to parliament. A number of deficiencies and distortions in the income tax regime involving both policy and administrative issues were to be addressed with the changes. Unfortunately, during parliamentary consideration, further retrograde changes were proposed with the opposite effect, and accordingly the package is stalled.

Key Conclusions

According to the PEFA assessment in 2007, Jordan's PFM system was performing well overall and its systems are clearly among the strongest in the region. The recent review by the Fund and Bank confirms that PFM reform has achieved notable successes. However, progress to date has been uneven despite considerable effort from the GoJ and extensive amounts of donor assistance. To some extent this may have been due to an underestimation by certain senior PFM officials of the challenges that confronted the effective implementation of a program of significant change. However, an important lesson from the Jordan case has been the institutional fragmentation of the budget process between MOF, GBD, MOP, and the 'Prime Minister's office which has been an obstacle in ensuring effective leadership of the reform process.

Annex: Jordan PEFA Assessment

Table 8A.1. Overview of the Performance Indicator Set

Indicator	MENA Regional PEFA Study 2010	Grade
Credibility of the budget	Aggregate expenditure out-turn compared to original approved budget	A
	Composition of expenditure out-turn compared to original approved budget	D
	Aggregate revenue out-turn compared to original approved budget	A
	Stock and monitoring of expenditure payment arrears	D
Comprehensiveness and transparency	Classification of the budget	A
	Comprehensiveness of information included in budget documentation	A
	Extent of unreported government operations	B
	Transparency of intergovernmental fiscal relations	B+
	Oversight of aggregate fiscal risk from other public sector entities	B+
	Public access to key fiscal information	B
Policy-based budgeting	Orderliness and participation in the annual budget process	B+
	Multiyear perspective in fiscal planning, expenditure policy, and budgeting	B+
Predictability and control in budget execution	Transparency of taxpayer obligations and liabilities	B
	Effectiveness of measures for taxpayer registration and tax assessment	C+
	Effectiveness in collection of tax payments	B
	Predictability in the availability of funds for commitment of expenditures	A
	Recording and management of cash balances, debt, and guarantees	B+
	Effectiveness of payroll controls	B
	Competition, value for money, and controls in procurement	B
	Effectiveness of internal controls for nonsalary expenditure	B
	Effectiveness of internal audit	C
Accounting, recording, and reporting	Timeliness and regularity of accounts reconciliation	B+
	Availability of information on resources received by service delivery units	D
	Quality and timeliness of in-year budget reports	C
	Quality and timeliness of annual financial statements	C
External scrutiny and audit	Scope, nature, and follow-up of external audit	C
	Legislative scrutiny of the annual budget law	A
	Legislative scrutiny of external audit reports	C
Donor practices	Predictability of direct budget support	C
	Financial information provided by donors for budgeting and reporting on project and program aid	D
	Proportion of aid that is managed by use of national procedures	D

Source: World Bank.

Notes

1. European Commission, *Jordan Public Expenditure Financial Assessment*, 2007.
2. World Bank/IMF, *Jordan: Advancing the PFM Reform Agenda*, 2009.
3. World Bank, *Progress Assessment in Introducing a Medium Term Expenditure Framework*, 2009.
4. The budget of 2008 has for the first time included the concept of "Results Oriented Budget," where the budget has included the vision of each ministry and government department as well as their mission, strategic objectives and programs to achieve these objectives, while being consistent with the national priorities that were included in the National Agenda and the Forum "We are all Jordan." Moreover indicators for measuring objectives and performance were developed to facilitate operations of expenditure monitoring and the verification of the efficiency of resource allocation. (*Source:* MOF website.)
5. World Bank/IMF, *Work Program for Consolidating Budget Management Reforms*, 2004.

One way out of this bind is to find a "compensation mechanism." Another is to promote a comprehensive package that would bring the whole system to a new equilibrium. Unfortunately, based on the current political environment in the economy, the opportunity for a comprehensive approach to reform is not readily foreseeable in the near future.

Key Conclusions

PFM reform in Lebanon has been a challenging endeavor. Some progress has been made in tax administration reform, but this is an exception. The approach to tax reform successfully blended international expertise with local ownership. The reforms—which targeted the critical issue of enhancing Government revenues—were sustainable, particularly with regard to the implementation of the value added tax. On the expenditure side, different implementation strategies have been followed and these have been less successful in generating ownership. However, the main factor behind the repeated failure to reform various elements of the PFM system was the political agenda of the various players. Finding a strategy that addresses these political factors will be critical if Lebanon's PFM reforms are to be successful in the future.

Notes

1. Public enterprises are considered part of the public sector by the IMF GFS 2001 Manual. Government oversight of aggregate fiscal risk from public sector entities is also included as a performance indicator by the PEFA under budget comprehensiveness and transparency.
2. According to the 1963 Public Accounting Law, all public funds have to be deposited at the Treasury Single Account (TSA) at the Banque du Liban (BDL). During the civil war, the law was modified to allow public agencies and municipalities to open separate accounts, although still at the BDL.
3. Lebanon remains one of the few economies in MENA that have neither signed nor ratified the UN Convention against Corruption (UNCAC).

CHAPTER 10

Morocco

David Shand
Daniel Tommasi

General Overview

Morocco is a lower-middle-income economy with a population estimated at 31.3 million in 2008. Its 2007 GDP per capita is estimated at US$4,093 in purchasing power parity (PPP) terms and US$2,422 in nominal terms. It gained full independence from France in 1956. It is a constitutional monarchy, although the King retains significant executive power. He appoints the Prime Minister and Cabinet based on election results. Opposition parties were allowed to take power after the 1998 elections. The new King, Mohammed VI, has moved the economy gradually towards greater democracy and freedom of expression. Further changes were made to the electoral system in the wake of the political protests in the region during 2011 that increase the power of the government while retaining a key role for the monarchy. There is an active and well established civil society.

The government is pursuing liberalization of the economy to improve the investment climate and attract foreign investment. Reform of the public sector is associated with this policy. Structural reforms have contributed to strong economic growth over the past decade. The economy is divided into 16 regions and some 61 provinces and prefectures, which have their own elected assemblies and budget. There are also around 1,500 communes.

Morocco's public financial management (PFM) system follows the French system. It has a solid legal basis which is strictly observed and provides strong central oversight of public finances. According to the most recent International Monetary Fund (IMF) Report on the Observance of Standards and Codes (ROSC), the PFM system is robust in terms of financial control and provides reliable information. Fiscal transparency is reasonable, but the scope of the budget needs expansion. Budget execution and accounting procedures are cumbersome and need streamlining.

Along with Tunisia, Morocco's scores are among the highest in the region on various dimensions of budgetary and financial management. The Bank's 2003 Country Financial Accountability Assessment (CFAAs) assessed Morocco's PFM fiduciary risk as low. Morocco has achieved success since 2003 in fiscal consolidation based on improved revenue management and stricter control of the civil service payroll, including the introduction of a voluntary retirement package in 2005. This consolidation has been achieved despite increases in international fuel and food prices, which have increased the burden of fuel and food subsidies in the budget. Morocco's fiscal targets for 2009—which include a budget deficit of no more than 3 percent of GDP, public debt of no more than 60 percent, and a civil service wage bill of less than 10 percent of GDP—have been achieved. The budget deficit was reduced from 5.2 percent of GDP in 2005 to 2 percent in 2006 and ernment and private sector employees, and civil servant health insurance) and some 220 autonomous government agencies, including the Hassan II Fund for Economic and Social Development. This fund receives a substantial proportion (up to 50 percent) of privatization revenues to finance economic, infrastructure and social projects. Its revenues and expenditures, which are around 6 percent of the investment budget outlays, are not included in the annual budget law or in the overall balance of central government. There is, however, some disclosure of its operations. The budget documents include a separate report on public establishments and enterprises, as discussed later. The PEFA assessment notes that, despite the extent of extra-budgetary funds, the amount of expenditures not covered in different fiscal reports is very small—less than one percent. Extra-budgetary funds are included in the Treasury Single Account.

The budget itself is somewhat fragmented, although the total picture is presented in a consolidated budget document. Under the Organic Budget Law, the budget is broken down into four separate components—the general budget covering ministries and related bodies and comprising about 85 percent of budget expenditures; 160 autonomous agencies or SEGMA (mainly educational institutions and hospitals); nearly 100 special Treasury accounts, including various earmarked revenues such as for roads and certain housing expenditures (which are exceptions to the Organic Budget Law provision of no earmarking or offsetting of revenues); and a fourth component comprised of various annexes that are now being abolished. Military expenditure is fully reported in the same way as expenditures of other ministries. All these components of the budget are executed according to the same rules.

The PEFA assessment rates the comprehensiveness of the budget documents as reasonable, noting that they contain five to six of the nine desirable pieces of information. This includes macroeconomic budget assumptions, budget balance, and financing information, stock of debt and major revenue and expenditure measures. Not included are financial assets and a summary of the prior year's information in comparable form.

The budget documents presented to Parliament are extensive. Apart from the draft budget law covering some 50 chapters and 10 annex tables, there is an economic and financial report providing macro-fiscal information, detailed budget booklets for each ministry's operating expenditures and staffing expenditures, and details of the other parts of the budget (autonomous agencies, special Treasury accounts and past and future financial operations of public establishments and state enterprises). While overall the budget information is extensive and available to the public, in practice, it is not user-friendly because of its fragmented nature. One particular deficiency is a lack of detailed information on budgeted and actual amounts for previous years.

The budget documents also contain an annex on the financial operations of state owned enterprises. The MEF exercises strong central oversight of these institutions through a separate MEF unit with several hundred staff. However, there does not appear to be any systematic management and reporting of contingent liabilities which arise from government guarantees of their financing. The scope of activity of state owned enterprises remains substantial, but their quasi-fiscal activities are limited. Social obligations carried out by these enterprises are generally covered by explicit payments to enterprises from the budget.

Contingent liabilities are not reported in the budget documents or elsewhere, with the exception of guarantees of external debt. On the other hand, there are no fewer than three separate reports published annually on the public debt. Since the 2007 budget, a report on tax expenditures has been included in the budget documents and published on the MEF website.

External financial assistance from international donors is included within the budget, with the exception of a few project-grants. Morocco has achieved a high degree of integration of project aid in the national system by setting up a reimbursement procedure. Expenditures financed from external aid are budgeted and paid by the Treasury according to the same procedure than other expenditures and the Treasury is then reimbursed by the donors. Therefore, expenditures financed from external aid are not separated from other expenditures in the budget documents. According to the MEF, all expenditures financed from external aid follow this reimbursement procedure with some exceptions, notably for some TA grants which are not covered by the budget.

Subnational governments (SNG) elect their own assemblies and develop their own budgets, which in the case of the provinces are executed by the governor who is appointed by the King and reports to the Ministry of Interior. The MEF and Ministry of the Interior must approve these budgets, and investment expenditures must reflect government priorities. Three revenue sources are shared with SNG, of which the 30 percent share of VAT revenues is the largest. The horizontal allocation of funds between SNG is largely determined by transparent mechanisms and rules. However, the level of transfers from central government is provided too late to SNG for them to fully take account of it in preparing their budget. While consolidated financial reports on SNG finances are prepared, they are generally too late to be useful—often over two years after the year end.

The 2005 IMF Fiscal ROSC concluded that parliamentary and public access to fiscal information is broadly satisfactory, although the information provided is complex and insufficiently standardized. The MEF has worked over the past four years to improve the provision of information to Parliament and the public. Budget execution is reported on a monthly basis (with a one month lag) in the official monthly Treasury statement. A six monthly budget execution report is provided to the Finance Committee of Parliament and is publicly available.

Thus overall, considerable fiscal information is publicly available including the budget documents, within year reports on budget execution, reports of the Court of Accounts and contract awards over a certain amount.

Policy-Based Budgeting. The budget cycle operates on a precise calendar established each year by a circular from the Prime Minister. Some delays have occurred, but the budget is invariably passed by Parliament before the commencement of the fiscal year.

The preparation of the budget is guided by broad policy orientations and priorities announced by the King and the Government. Apart from providing the macroeconomic context and fiscal targets, it contains sectoral objectives for designated priority sectors. The budget guidelines circular sets spending ceilings for each ministry based on these priorities.

Previously, a five year economic and social development plan used to be prepared and adopted by Parliament, establishing broad guidelines as well as expenditure projections based on macroeconomic projections. The last five year plan covered the period from 2000–04. This approach has now been discontinued.

The High Planning Commissariat has prepared a strategic note for 2007–15. This note provides broad policy orientations and identifies growth scenarios. The MEF has been preparing a three year rolling MTFF since 2007 to guide the expenditure ceilings. The focus now is on developing sector MTEFs as the basis for increased allocative efficiency. With the support of the Bank, an MTEF handbook was prepared in 2006. In 2008, nine sector/ministry MTEFs were prepared. The preparation of sector MTEFs is being extended to five additional ministries with the support of the Bank.

The MTEF handbook covers processes to ensure close integration between MTEF and budget preparation and framing the sector MTEFs within indicative expenditure ceilings for each sector. However, this integration with the budget has yet to be implemented, although this may occur in the 2009 budget, and the effectiveness of these sector MTEFs prepared in isolation from the budget is therefore unclear. All ministries have prepared 2008–12 action plans which are intended to guide the elaboration of sector MTEFs.

These MTEFs may improve allocative efficiency if their processes are integrated into the budget processes, as recommended in the methodological guide. Nevertheless, at the moment, preparation of the budget remains input based with little explicit discussion of policies and priorities.

Previously, the Bank was providing assistance to the government to develop a performance budgeting approach based on pilots in a number of ministries. However, while some performance budget documents were drafted, government support for this exercise was weak and the initiative has not been pursued after these initial drafts. (There have recently been some indications that this could be changing.) The budget documents include hundreds of input or output indicators, but little attention is paid to them. The government intends to improve these performance indicators, including reducing their number. The government has improved the presentation of the budget documents. The line-item classification has been streamlined, but further progress is required. Recurrent and investment expenditures of ministries are presented in separate volumes. Goods and service expenditures are detailed by ministry and directorate, but personnel expenditures are only detailed by ministry.

It is expected that these issues will be addressed under the implementation of the new Organic Budget Law. Performance budgeting will be a key item in the new Organic Budget Law, and the Government will implement a modern budget classification that has already been drafted.

A few performance contracts have been developed between the Ministry of Health and its de-concentrated regional divisions. In October 2009, 17 performance contracts have been signed with universities. It is premature to assess the impact of these contracts on budget management. There are also moves to provide the Inspectorate General of Finances with a performance auditing role, but the lack of technical capacity has limited progress.

Predictability and Control in Budget Execution. Tax administration continues to improve. The PEFA assessment ranks tax administration highly, noting the strict limits on discretionary powers of tax officials, easy taxpayer access to information to assist them in meeting their obligations and the existence of appeal mechanisms (although it is too early to assess the latter). The legal basis for taxes is clear and tax legislation is modern, albeit complex and frequently amended. A single taxpayer identification number is under development, as is a web based system for providing information to taxpayers and receiving declarations. Performance criteria for tax audits have been adopted and a government claims preparation code has been developed.

The budget execution system is well-structured and reliable to ensure the legal correctness of expenditures, but has been cumbersome and slow with an excessive level of ex ante controls. It takes considerable time for funds to be made available to spending ministries, although Special Treasury accounts and autonomous agencies may carry forward funds within specified limits. It also takes considerable time to enter into to commitments and to authorize payments. The commitment stage is complex, time consuming and subject to delays leading to approval and payment bottlenecks towards the end of the year. It reflects the strong controls of the French system with separate processes for commitment of expenditure, verification of payment and payment authorization on the one hand, and making payments and accounting on the other.

A prior action for the 2008 DPL was the simplification of ex ante controls to reduce paperwork and improve budget execution. In 2007, cumbersome virement rules were revised to provide greater flexibility to ministries. This has already resulted in improvement in the timeliness of budget execution. Morocco has embarked on a reform of the organization its ex ante control system. By a decree of February 2006, the *TGR* (Kingdom General Treasury), which controls payment orders, and the CGED (General Control of Expenditures Commitment), which controls commitments, have been merged. It is planned that ministerial treasuries, reporting to the MEF but located within ministries, will perform simplified modernized ex ante control, which will be based on risk assessments and the size of the transactions. For the moment, only a very few "ministerial treasuries" have been implemented.

The PEFA assessment suggests other significant recent improvements. It comments that cash planning is well carried out and that spending ministries are able to plan and commit expenditures consistent with their budget allocation at least six months in advance. While there are significant within year budget adjustments as discussed above, these are clear and transparent.

There is a strong system of internal audit comprising the Inspectorate-General of Finance (IGF), which conducts ex post audits, and the audit and inspection division of the Treasury within the MOF. There are also general inspection offices in individual ministries, but they are weaker than the IGF. The PEFA assessment comments that IGF observes international internal auditing standards, and thus focuses on systems improvement issues and not just compliance.

Accounting, Recording, and Reporting. Bank reconciliations in the central administration are carried out at least monthly. However, reconciliation of suspense accounts and advances is less satisfactory, being carried out only annually. In addition, a number of such accounts and advances remain un-reconciled.

Budget execution is reported on a monthly basis (with a one month lag) in the official monthly Treasury statement and enables direct comparison with the initial budget. The information is considered reliable. A biannual budget execution report is provided to the Finance Committee of Parliament and is publicly available.

Authorizing officers, accounting officers, and auditors have their own separate computer systems, which make it difficult to exchange data. However, a new integrated

Political Economy of Reform

The broader political environment has assisted the reforms. Public sector reform is seen as part of overall structural reform, and it does not seem that the PFM reform was affected by political developments such as elections. Rather, improved governance is central to the Government's economic and social reforms. Improving public sector operations, and particularly improving service delivery, is widely seen as an important objective.

The reform program was first launched by a Prime Minister order in 2002. The current Government's reform program was approved by Parliament in 2007. The then Prime Minister gave significant support. There is no clear opposition to the PFM reforms, but rather different points of view on its end objectives. The Budget Directorate (DB) has adopted a cautious approach, but it has implemented effectively discrete and concrete reforms. Line ministries are expecting increased responsibilities and flexibility in budget management and want more rapid and effective progress, but the DB has been reluctant to move too quickly on these issues.

There has been extensive consultation with civil society, in which the Bank has participated. Since 2002 the PARAP has been the topic of numerous debates, seminars, and conferences. This consultation has confirmed the direction of PARAP and added momentum to its implementation.

As mentioned earlier, managers of the MEF and DB have been clear on what they wished to achieve under the reforms and have controlled the pace of reform. Because they present the reform in an optimistic light, there is at times a mismatch between the way the reform measures are understood by the press and donors and the actual results on the ground. The DB has now agreed to prepare a new OBL, because of both the EC and the Bank pressures and discussion with its peers in France and other economies. If recent history is any guide, the approach is likely to remain cautious and incremental.

Morocco is not particularly dependent on foreign assistance, which represented 4.2 percent of the 2009 budget revenues (compared with 3.2 percent in 2005 and 3.8 percent in 2006 and 2007). These figures cover both budget support and project aid, but exclude some small amounts of grants which are outside the budget. Dialogue with the EC on PFM is seen as facilitating increased economic cooperation with the EC. Dialogue with the Bank may have an indirect effect on the dialogue with the EC.

France's and other OECD economies moves to reform their PFM have had some influence. Particularly, the approach developed in France to streamline the ex ante expenditure controls, based on a risk management approach, has influenced the Morocco's ongoing reform of ex ante financial control. It appears that, as compared with Algeria and Tunisia, Morocco is more open and inclined to following the French approach in such an area.

Key Conclusions

The pace of reform has been set by the economy itself, and this has resulted in a number of modest but effective reforms. However, it is expected that with the OBL under preparation, the reform process will be deepened. It remains to be seen whether the pace of reform will accelerate and gain greater traction, or continue to move at a steady pace. In any case, the development of an effective performance oriented approach to budgeting needs time.

Annex: Morocco PEFA Assessment

Table 10A.1. Overview of the Performance Indicator Set

Indicator	MENA Regional PEFA Study 2010	Grade
Credibility of the budget	Aggregate expenditure out-turn compared to original approved budget	A
	Composition of expenditure out-turn compared to original approved budget	C
	Aggregate revenue out-turn compared to original approved budget	A
	Stock and monitoring of expenditure payment arrears	C+
Comprehensiveness and transparency	Classification of the budget	A
	Comprehensiveness of information included in budget documentation	B
	Extent of unreported government operations	C+
	Transparency of intergovernmental fiscal relations	C
	Oversight of aggregate fiscal risk from other public sector entities	B
	Public access to key fiscal information	A
Policy-based budgeting	Orderliness and participation in the annual budget process	A
	Multiyear perspective in fiscal planning, expenditure policy, and budgeting	C+
Predictability and control in budget execution	Transparency of taxpayer obligations and liabilities	A
	Effectiveness of measures for taxpayer registration and tax assessment	B+
	Effectiveness in collection of tax payments	B+
	Predictability in the availability of funds for commitment of expenditures	C+
	Recording and management of cash balances, debt, and guarantees	A
	Effectiveness of payroll controls	B+
	Competition, value for money, and controls in procurement	B
	Effectiveness of internal controls for nonsalary expenditure	C+
	Effectiveness of internal audit	C+
Accounting, recording, and reporting	Timeliness and regularity of accounts reconciliation	A
	Availability of information on resources received by service delivery units	B
	Quality and timeliness of in-year budget reports	B+
	Quality and timeliness of annual financial statements	D+
External scrutiny and audit	Scope, nature, and follow-up of external audit	D+
	Legislative scrutiny of the annual budget law	B+
	Legislative scrutiny of external audit reports	D+
Donor practices	Predictability of direct budget support	Not Rated
	Financial information provided by donors for budgeting and reporting on project and program aid	D+
	Proportion of aid that is managed by use of national procedures	B

Source: World Bank.

CHAPTER 11

The Syrian Arab Republic

Mark Ahern

General Overview

In the past decade, the Syrian Arab Republic has embarked on a transition from a centrally planned to a "social market" economy. The public financial management (PFM) system is starting to change in line with the change in economic approach, but many of the features of the system from the central planning period remain to date.

Within the government, PFM is led by the Ministry of Finance (MOF) and the State Planning Commission (SPC), although the SPC role has been diminished with the transfer of responsibility for the investment budget to MOF in 2008. The Central Organization for Financial Control (COFC) operates as Syria's supreme audit institution. The PFM system is dominated by the central government, but the offices of line ministries located in the governorates are financed through the Ministry of Local Administration. The Governors oversee the administration of these resources but do not have an active role in allocating resources to the offices in their governorate.

In recent years a number of reforms have been instigated with the support of the former Deputy Prime Minister (who is a former United Nations official) and the Minister of Finance. As part of this process, a major review of the PFM system was carried out by a joint mission of the World Bank and the International Monetary Fund (IMF) in early 2006. This review provides the most comprehensive assessment of the current PFM system. Although the report set out a possible strategy for reform of the system, the Government has not adopted a reform strategy. The World Bank conducted limited further work in the PFM area following this study, but in the past year the Bank has started a more active dialogue with the Syrian authorities as part of a wider governance agenda. Since 2006, the IMF has continued to play a minor role with technical assistance (TA) in the area of budget preparation. The IMF has had a larger involvement with the Ministry of Finance (MOF) on revenue administration reform, which is a priority of the Minister of Finance.

The European Union (EU) started a large project in the MOF in 2005 (known as the MOF Modernization project) with tax administration and customs components, along with a component in the PFM field. The PFM elements of the project focused on budget classification, accounting, and performance budgeting issues. The EU is about to launch a successor project in 2010. The United Nations (UN) agencies have been active in Syria covering most sectors, however they have not been working in the MOF nor had an active role on PFM issues.

Substantive Reform Agenda

An informal Public Expenditure Financial Accountability (PEFA) assessment was completed alongside the 2006 World Bank/IMF report but was not widely disseminated. A summary of the performance PEFA indicator scores can be found in the annex to this chapter. Using a four-point rating scale, the assessment produces the results shown in table 11.1.

Table 11.1. Syrian Arab Republic Abbreviated Summary of PEFA Indicator Scores

PEFA Score	Number of Indicators
A (best)	0
B	4
C	10
D (worst)	10
Not Rated	7[a]
Total	31[b]

Source: World Bank.
Note: a. There are 3 donor and the 3 tax administration indicators that form part of the PEFA framework.
b. PEFA comprises 28 system indicators and 3 donor indicators.

The EU is proposing that a full PEFA assessment be undertaken at the start of the new project in 2010—with an aim that it clarify priorities for the new project. The following sections set out the reform agenda in each of the six sections of the PEFA framework.

Credibility of the Budget. In Syria, the budget is a compliance document rather than central element of fiscal management. When comparing the execution of the budget in Syria against the original presentation, the revenue projections have proven to be broadly accurate. However, the expenditure outturn frequently differs significantly from the original budget. The variance on the expenditure side in part reflects the secondary role played by the budget in fiscal management. Policy decisions are largely taken outside the budget cycle, and the budget process is a technical exercise that attempts to reconcile the policy decisions with determined fiscal constraints. In the process, there is limited connection between an agreed policy and the budget provision, which can result in significant changes to the budget during implementation. Although the World Bank/IMF report proposed major reforms to the budget preparation process, there have not been any reforms to increase the relevance of the budget in fiscal management to date.

Comprehensiveness and Transparency. The budget documents are prepared for the specific purpose of parliamentary discussion, and they are not generally available to the public. They focus on line item allocations but contain limited information on the overall fiscal position, or the government's expenditure priorities. The budget covers all expenditure of administrative entities and any transfers to economic entities, but the boundary between administrative and economic entities is not clear. Although the EU prepared a revised budget classification in 2008 (including an economic classification in line with the GFS 2001 classification), it is not clear that the existing IT system has sufficient flexibility in the chart of accounts to manage the new classification, and there has been no attempt to implement it.

Policy-Based Budgeting. The five year plan is the main planning process and includes medium term fiscal projections prepared by the SPC. The German development agency GTZ has in the past been involved in supporting capacity development of modeling at SPC for the five year plan. There has been no macro-fiscal analysis or forecasting for the annual budget. Following a recommendation of the IMF, the MOF intends to establish a small team in the Budget Department to prepare fiscal projections.

The responsibility for the investment budget was shifted from the SPC to the MOF in 2008, and the MOF had this responsibility during the preparation of the 2009 Budget. Despite responsibility for the investment budget moving to the MOF, the separation of the two budgets was maintained within the MOF. In the line ministries, there are separate planning and finance departments with responsibility for the investment and recurrent budgets, respectively.

The EU MOF Modernization project conducted a number of training workshops for the budget department on performance budgeting concepts, but no reforms were made on the back of this training. The IMF is providing support to the budget department with medium term forward estimates. The work is focusing on two pilot ministries and utilizes a program structure to integrate the recurrent and investment budgets. The work started in 2007, and it is intended that the presentation of the 2010 budget would include forward estimates for the two pilot ministries using the program structure.

Predictability and Control in Budget Execution. There is a heavy emphasis on transaction control in the Syrian system. The MOF financial controllers are involved in ex ante control of transactions and the COFC scrutinizes ex post. There is an internal audit operation for all government entities linked to the central inspection agency (CACI), but the function does not meet recognized professional standards. The heavy focus on control makes the budget execution process extremely rigid, but to date there is not a reform program in this area.

The authorities amended the legal environment for procurement with the Uniform System of Contracts Law No (51) of 2004, which was enacted in 2005. In commenting on the procurement system, the 2006 World Bank/IMF report noted that there are a number of features of the current procurement system that limit the level of competition for contracts. In particular, there are explicit preferences provided to state enterprises, single sourcing is commonly used, and there are no defined processes for addressing complaints. In 2008, the authorities asked the World Bank to complete an assessment of the procurement system using the Country Procurement Assessment Report (CPAR) methodology, and it is possible that a reform agenda will emerge from this assessment.

The responsibility for managing the government's funds is divided between the Treasury Department and the Public Debt Department in the MOF. The Treasury manages funds associated with budget expenditure, while the Public Debt Department manages a Fund that is financed from debt issuance and the proceeds of surpluses from state enterprises. This fund is used to make investments into state enterprises. The World Bank/IMF report recommended that the two departments be restructured so that they have clearly defined roles and responsibilities—with the Treasury being responsible for financing of the public sector's needs and the management of these funds. The government has not acted on this recommendation.

Accounting, Recording, and Reporting. Budget execution is managed through a network of financial directorates, with a directorate in each governorate. All of the directorates now have an information technology (IT) system to manage the execution process, with the final three directorates automated in October 2009. However, there is no network linking the IT systems of the financial directorates, and any reports to Damascus are provided in hard copy. In year reporting is confined to the investment budget, and while there are various reports on transactions, there is no comprehensive fiscal reporting.

The EU MOF Modernization project developed an Iraq Financial Management Information System (IFMIS) to support budget monitoring. The intention was that the system would operate only at the MOF and would receive information from the financial directorates, which would continue to execute the budget using existing systems. The system was developed over two years and was completed in 2008, but it is not being used by the MOF.

The Syrian accounting system operates on a single entry basis. The EU project was meant to support the introduction of double entry accounting. The strategy adopted was to incorporate updated accounting procedures in the IFMIS as it is being developed. As the IFMIS is not being used, the approach has had no impact.

External Scrutiny and Audit. The external audit agency (COFC) carries out audits of all public bodies as well as state enterprises. Its focus is on transaction level testing rather than risk assessments. The agency is a member of the International Organization of Supreme Audit Institutions (INTOSAI). The COFC reports are submitted to the People's Assembly, but appear to have little impact. There are no current plans to reform the activity of the agency.

Summary. The main success in reforming the PFM system has been the transfer of responsibility for the investment budget to the MOF from the SPC. This has integrated the budget management process in the MOF—although it has to date been a relocation exercise, and the opportunity to reform the budget process in light of this change has yet to be fully grasped.

Although the EU MOF Modernization project aimed to address a number of important weaknesses in the PFM system, the outcomes of this project were limited. Many activities were undertaken by the project team, but the work was not integrated into the operations of the relevant line departments in the MOF. Moreover, the strategy adopted attempted to overcome the capacity weaknesses in the civil service by incorporating the new approaches (such as double entry accounting) into a new IFMIS that the project was developing at the MOF. As the IFMIS is not being used by the MOF, these efforts have failed. The EU is looking to refocus the successor project to improve its effectiveness.

The PFM reform agenda has so far been limited. In general, the initiatives have been focused on the MOF but have been relatively discrete. Although many PFM reforms would have an impact well beyond the MOF, there has been little if any discussion of the possible reforms with other agencies, or with other ministers, to date.

Implementation Strategies for Reform

Although the 2006 World Bank/IMF report presented a possible action plan for reforms, this was never discussed by the government and has had limited visibility. The decision to transfer the investment budget to the MOF was driven by the minister in charge of the SPC (the current Deputy Prime Minister) and was not linked to a broader PFM reform strategy.

The EU MOF Modernization project determined its priorities based on an initial assessment of Syria's PFM systems. While these priorities were endorsed by the senior managers of the MOF in their role overseeing the project, it does not appear that the reforms were given a high priority by the MOF. The MOF manager charged with overseeing the EU MOF Modernization project was an advisor to the minister (and more recently has been appointed the Manager of International Relations). The project was managed outside the MOF, and the line managers within the MOF were not closely involved on a day to day basis. There was a formal process for monitoring the project with regular reports on activities. But given the limited achievements of the project, it does not appear that this process was effective.

The IMF has been working directly with the Budget Directorate, although the Deputy Minister of Finance follows developments. While there were few signs of progress in the early stages of the project, there is now a prospect of some reform being reflected in the 2010 budget process. Although the IMF is following developments, there is no mechanism for monitoring progress within the MOF.

Both the EU and the IMF have offered staff workshops and study tours to increase their understanding of the proposed reforms they were promoting. These were welcomed by the staff concerned, but had no discernible impact on progress with the reform.

The revenue administration reforms being pursued by the government have involved establishing a new revenue agency that is not subject to the standard civil service regulations. This should allow more flexibility in remuneration, which is considered to be an important feature in motivating the staff of the new agency.

It is too early to comment on the success of piloting of reforms. The IMF project with the budget department aims to pilot the forward estimates techniques with two ministries in the 2010 budget, and this will be an opportunity to assess the approach.

Political Economy of Reform

Syrian politics has been dominated by the ruling Baath party for many decades. While this has created a stable environment, the lack of reforms over a long period has made the civil service extremely cautious when considering change.

The push for reform in Syria has come from the highest political level, with the main proponents in the PFM area being the Deputy Prime Minister and the Minister of Finance. Over the past five years, these two key reformers have retained their position, which has helped provide continuity to the reform effort. Senior civil servants in the MOF and the SPC have been responding to directions from Ministers and have not been active proponents. Broader geopolitical developments have exerted tremendous pressure on Syria and occasionally diverted the attention of the key political figures.

The capacity to manage reforms within the civil service is weak. There is enthusiasm from junior staff, but within a hierarchical civil service, this has limited effect. The lack of leadership from the senior civil service is a significant constraint on the ambitions of the Ministers. In view of this, the Minister of Finance has focused his efforts, giving priority to reforms in tax administration over those of expenditure management.

Because the Syrian PFM system has changed little over an extensive period, there is no real culture of reform within the civil service. This factor, coupled with a heavy control environment that has historically discouraged innovation, has created a very challenging environment for reform. However, in general the civil service has provided passive support rather than an active campaign of resistance against proposed changes. In addition, there are some in the ruling party who are suspicious of changes that they consider to be promoted from outside, such as the proposals to reform the PFM system. This may explain why a low key approach has been taken to such reforms in the past.

Syria has not been aid dependent, and as a consequence the donors have not been influential. The EU has been negotiating an Association Agreement as part of its neighborhood policy, but the Agreement has not been ratified. The UN agencies have been active providing technical assistance in a range of sectors, but they have not been involved in PFM reform. The World Bank has not been active in Syria for a number of years and is considered by some non-reformers to be a tool of those exerting pressure on the economy.

Key Conclusions

To date, the attempts at PFM reform in Syria have not been successful. The capacity to manage PFM reform is limited, and any change requires a concerted political effort and focused support. The Minister of Finance has responded to the capacity constraints by focusing specifically on revenue reforms. The Minister's support, coupled with incentives for staff created by the establishment of a new revenue agency with more remuneration flexibility, has led to some progress in this area. However, progress has been slower than planned, with a delay in the planned introduction of a value added tax (VAT).

The efforts on expenditure reforms were primarily led by donors, and there has been limited ownership by the authorities to date. The projects were implemented without the government discussing expenditure reform objectives and without an agreed reform strategy. Moreover, the EU MOF Modernization project was not closely linked to the work of the line managers in the MOF. The donor projects therefore developed little traction and did not have a direct impact on the PFM system, although they may have prepared important ground for future initiatives.

all deviation in primary expenditure by 10 percent in only one year, and that actual revenues consistently exceeded budget revenues with the largest variation being over 13 percent in 2008. The variation in investment expenditures was generally higher than that for recurrent expenditures, but not significantly so. This is due to the authorities' practice to keep a reserve of unallocated investment spending of around 10 percent in order to compensate the limited flexibility of their five-year development plan. Important changes to the initially approved budget are done in a transparent manner through a modified appropriation act, as was the case twice during the last three years.

Aggregate budget execution data and the initial budget are set out in the *Official Gazette,* which is published on the MOF website annually about three months after year end thus enabling comparison at the aggregate level (table 12.1). Quarterly budget execution data is also available on the IMF Special Data Dissemination Standards (SDSS). The final accounts (*Loi de Règlement*) and the 2006 initial budget are also on the website, but comparison of actual versus budget in terms of expenditure composition may be difficult because of differing formats.

Table 12.1. Budget Execution Rates

	2006			2007			2008		
	Est.	Act.	%	Est.	Act.	%	Est.	Act.	%
Operating expenditures	7,076	7,112	100.5	7,606	7,904	104	8,528	9,341	109.5
Investment expenditures from general revenue	2,068	2,109	101.9	2,295	2,566	111.7	2,558	2,721	106.4
Total	**9,144**	**9,221**	**100.8**	**9,901**	**10,471**	**105.7**	**11,086**	**12,062**	**108.8**

Source: MOF.

Expenditure arrears do not seem to be an issue, given the constant treasury surplus, the robust budget control systems in place and the regulation providing compensation for late payments to suppliers.

Comprehensiveness and Transparency. The budget classification system is not fully compliant with GFS 2001, particularly because of the absence of a functional classification. The classification system in some cases mixes administrative with input (economic) categories, as noted by the DPR.

Budget coverage is generally comprehensive. The CFAA notes that off-budget funds do exist and that the budget also excludes the operations of the social security funds. However, all donor project loans are included in the budget although donor project grants are not. As mentioned below, the revenues and expenditures of many funds/agencies that are off budget are shown as information in the budget documents. In the agriculture sector, professional offices (*offices des céréales*) managed by professional organizations are off-budget. But this may be explained by their governance arrangements.

The MOF coordinates the preparation of both the recurrent and investment components of the budget (title I and title II). Generally, a new investment project may be included in the budget only if it is included in the five year development plan, which is prepared by the MDCI. However there are a few exceptions for Presidential decisions. The development plan therefore represents a pre-selection of investment projects, but not all planned projects are budgeted. To ensure that the new investment budgeted projects are in conformity with the planned policies the Ministry of Development and

International Cooperation (MDCI) participates as policy advisor in budget discussions held between the MOF and line ministries. Other central institutions involved in PFM, such as the Ministry of Civil Service and the Directorate General of Financial Control, may also participate.

The main limitation on the comprehensiveness and the quality of budget documents, as underlined in the CFAA, is that they do not give a complete picture of public spending. They cover only central government ministry revenue and expenditure, with separate booklets giving details on spending by public enterprises or entities receiving transfers from the budget. Local government budgets and the social security funds are not covered by government fiscal data. The former represent around 5 percent of the central budget. However the budget documents show expenditures financed by own source revenues of several public agencies, including transfers from the social security institutions to the public hospitals. The government financial table produced by the MOF has the same coverage than the budget documents. Some data covering the whole general government is published on the SDDS, but the data is not timely and is of questionable quality.

Some revenues and expenditures are managed through Special Treasury Funds, defined by the Organic Budget Law. These represented 3.7 percent of the 2009 initial budget. They constitute an exception to the principle of non-earmarking of revenue and to the principle of annual expiration, as their balances are automatically carried over from one year to the next. In addition, their management is more flexible than other budget appropriations, since their expenditure ceiling may be raised during the year if revenue is higher than budgeted. However, their operations are transparent in that their receipts, expenditure, and balances are recorded in the annual budget laws and are detailed in the budget documents.

Capital expenditures are partly de-concentrated to the governorate level. The 2004 CFAA comments that the transparency of budgetary relations between central and local government could be improved and suggests an annual summary of revenue sharing should be included as an annex to the budget.

In terms of oversight of fiscal risk, the CFAA noted that government guarantees for borrowing by public entities are not systematically managed and disclosed, but their amounts are minimal compared to the size of the budget. However, the aggregate amount of government guarantees is now disclosed in the debt annual report published on the MOF web site six months after the end of the year. Furthermore, the Prime Minister's Office and the Court of Accounts ensure that all autonomous agencies and public enterprises prepare audited annual financial statements, which are centrally reviewed in terms of fiscal risks, including by the MOF.

According to the CFAA, the documents that make up the budget law and its annexes are well prepared, easy to understand, and contain much relevant information. Most of the information requirements for budget documentation in the PEFA methodology seem to be met, but this will be addressed by the forthcoming PEFA assessment. The overview that introduces the budget law and the report on budget data provide good information. The economic and financial overview prepared by MCDI (termed the economic budget) is well written and illustrated with numerous macroeconomic tables in support of the assumptions on which the budget is based. However, the projections are for only one year forward. The same is true of the budget summary, which includes revenue tables

2008. It was reviewed in detail and completed by high level MOF officials at the request of the Minister of Finance in the second quarter of 2009. It is expected that it will be further reviewed in the Inter-ministerial Committee chaired by the Prime Minister. Although it has not been formally approved by the government, it has been largely used in the reform implementation as well as included in the EC budget support to the reform, with which it was closely coordinated.

This draft master plan gives broad objectives and directions for the reform. It also details some measures to be implemented in a pilot period that will involve a few ministries, focusing for the moment on the implementation of sector MTEFs (which will be, in principle, framed by an aggregate MTFF and a Medium Term Budget Framework (MTBF) that will frame the inter-sectoral resource allocation) and performance monitoring. It covers a range of PFM issues and includes a proposed training program, the implementation of a new budget classification, the finalization of the chart of accounts and the preparation of a new organic budget law. The master plan suggests studies of possible streamlining of budget execution procedures but remains non-committal. While such a reform may be supported by the MOF and line ministries officials, as it would make line ministries more responsible and accountable, it may face resistance from the financial comptrollers who report to the Prime Minister. The roll-out of the reform beyond pilot ministries would start around 2015 with the enactment of a new organic budget law and the implementation of a new budget classification.

The key player in PFM reform is the MOF, which contains a small general directorate dedicated to the reforms—the GBO (budget management by objectives) MOF unit. Similar GBO units have been established in the pilot ministries. The MOF GBO unit does not produce regular progress reports, but since 2007–08 it has prepared reports as requested by the Finance Minister or the Prime Minister.

It is too early to discuss successes or failures of the current reform program. Until mid-2007 almost no progress had been achieved in PFM reform. Since then, progress has been made, although at a slow pace. The draft reform master plan provides a vision of the reform scope and defines the first steps in the reform process. However, the government prefers to await the results of the pilots and the various studies proposed by the draft master plan before deciding on a number of key issues, such as the reform of the budget execution system.

Initially, three ministries and a division of the Ministry of Education have been selected as pilots for the MTEF and performance budgeting initiative. The 2008 agreement with the EC provides for three additional pilot ministries in 2010. The whole Ministry of Education has been made pilot in late 2009, at the request of its minister and staff. The Bank and the EC will provide technical assistance in these pilots.

Achieving progress in these pilots will need constant input and attention. While program managers should play a major role in the development of a performance pilot budgeting approach, for the moment their status is unclear and no financial or other incentives have been provided to them. In the same way, for the moment, the GBO units established within line ministries are ill-equipped, insufficiently staffed, and have not been provided with any particular incentives.

The MTEF and performance budgeting pilots could be either self reinforcing or self defeating, depending on which extent they will feed into the budgeting process and whether they will provide other benefits to line ministries, such as increased flexibility in budget management.

Political Economy of Reform

The broader political environment has helped the reform. PFM reform was a key measure in the 2004 Presidential program, which was the origin of the reforms, and most politicians support PFM reform. The slow pace of reform could raise some doubts on the political commitment, despite the 2004 Presidential program, its integration in the XIth Development Plan and the recent developments noted above. The new Presidential program issued in October 2009 focuses more on the accounting reform as well as on other public administration reforms (such as e-governance and public service quality) rather than budget reforms. This does not mean that budget reform will stop, but it appears to not be enjoying the same degree of high-level attention it enjoyed earlier.

In addition, a large part of Tunisian society expects movement in the direction of European standards for public management, reflecting Tunisia's desire to converge more towards the EU. The Government's commitment to improve economic competitiveness and attract foreign investment recognizes the importance of a well functioning public sector, as set out in the *Strategy for the Development of the Public Service 2007–11*.

Most senior officials in the MOF appear now to be committed to PFM reform. Prior to 2007, while many senior officials supported the reform, some senior and well-positioned officials seemed reluctant to facilitate progress. In a workshop on the reform experience held in June 2006, for example, the then Minister of Finance called for extreme caution in implementing the reform. The situation changed in 2007. The new manager of the MOF GBO is clearly committed to reform implementation, and the Minister of Finance has played an active role in finalizing the draft reform master plan.

Within the pilot ministries, enthusiasm for PFM reform was uneven until 2008. It has increased significantly in 2009. Although some officials believe that cooperation between MOF and line ministries would benefit from improvement, progress has been made recently and solid cooperation has been achieved between the MOF and GBO units in line ministries. Budget execution reforms may face resistance from the financial comptrollers, who report to the Prime Minister's Office, since they may fear losing their power if ex ante financial controls are relaxed. However, they may agree with such reforms if a gradual approach is adopted or if their duties evolve with the reform.

Within line ministries, the reform may face opposition from those who fear losing their powers because of the introduction of management by program. It is still premature to assess which groups within line ministries will be affected. However, some general directors who will not be appointed as program managers, as well as the financial and planning departments in some line ministries, may fear losing their status and influence with the implementation of a program approach. Governors may also fear some loss of power under if sectoral MTEFs and performance budgeting are implemented. PFM reforms will need to be carefully designed and managed to limit this potential resistance. It does not appear that the powerful agriculture regional commissioners will lose power, and they appear to favor reform.

Taking into account previous experience, such as the hospital performance contracts, some are skeptical that a performance based approach will achieve necessary changes. However, performance contracts have been implemented recently in the Higher Education sector, and the Ministries of Education and Health are considering moving in this direction. It is premature to assess whether the lessons from the failed previous experiences in implementing performance contracts will be duly taken into account. However, performance contracting and performance budgeting need to be implemented hand in hand.

Current dissatisfaction and future resistance may be analyzed in parallel. For example, managers within line ministries complain about intrusive activities of financial comptroller controls or about regional commissioners who do not implement subsector polices. However, the level of dissatisfaction is comparatively low, while reform credibility is gaining ground in light of the recent progress.

Key Conclusions

Within Tunisia, the key issue is political commitment. The fact that PFM reform is included in the XIth Development Plan but not in the new Presidential political program does not mean that the reforms will be halted. Nevertheless, it will not facilitate its implementation, especially because the reform was included in the previous presidential program, and it may inadvertently signal that these reforms have slipped as a priority at the highest political level. However, there have been several positive developments as well. Pilot ministries have been increasingly involved and are now committed to undertaking new PFM approaches. The MOF GBO (reform) unit is active and the draft reform master plan has been widely reviewed and followed within the MOF. Furthermore, parallel reforms (such as accounting reform and performance contracting) might reinforce the main budget reform, which offers an opportunity to modernize the current PFM system, irrespective of how strong the link between performance and the budget might be.

However, incentives for the reform may be tempered by the fact that dissatisfaction with the current system is weak and it is unclear if there will be quick wins. Resistance from the financial controllers and other technicians may exist, but they are not the key challenges. MTEF and performance reports will probably be produced by the pilot ministries and the reform program agreed with EC will generally be implemented. However, without strong political support and the delegation of greater responsibility for PFM reform to program heads and managers, there is a risk that such activities may be largely technocratic and bureaucratic in nature. The key issue remains as to whether a broad consensus can be built on these reforms and to what extent they will actually improve government decision making processes.

Notes

1. World Bank, *Tunisia Country Governance Brief*, 2008.
2. S. Schiavo Campo, *Tunisia Development Policy Review*, 2008.

CHAPTER 13

The West Bank and Gaza

Mark Ahern

General Overview

The Palestinian Authority (PA) was established in 1994 following the 1993 Oslo Agreement, with responsibility for areas of the West Bank and Gaza under Palestinian control.[1] The PA adopted a public financial management (PFM) system which broadly follows the Anglo model, but in the 10 years following the Oslo Agreement the PFM system evolved. Authority became increasingly concentrated in the executive, and the role of the parliament was reduced. Within the executive, the president dominated, collective decision making was limited, and institutional arrangements were weak.

With the start of the second *intifada* in 2000, the PA's finances deteriorated significantly. The government was pressured by donors to initiate a range of reforms—including reform of the PFM system. These reforms started in 2002, with Salam Fayyad as the new Minister of Finance, and the first stage continued through 2005. The broad aim of these reforms was to improve expenditure control and oversight of PA resources. They ended up being among the most far-reaching of those implemented in the Middle East and North Africa (MENA) region during the last decade.

Following the election of a Hamas government in 2006 and the re-imposition of budgetary restrictions by Israel and donors, a further fiscal crisis ensued and a number of the PFM procedures and practices stopped operating. A second stage of reforms (initially aimed at reestablishing the systems in place in 2005) commenced with the formation of a Caretaker Government led by Salam Fayyad in mid-2007. Because the Caretaker Government did not have effective control of Gaza, these reforms also involved establishing institutions in the West Bank to replace those previously operating in Gaza.

Important agencies in the reform process are the Ministry of Finance (MOF), the Ministry of Planning (MOP), and the Palestine Investment Fund (or PIF, which is responsible for the oversight of state enterprises). In 2005, the State Audit and Administrative Control Bureau (SAACB) was established with an external audit function—although this entity had a minimal role before 2008.

A large number of donors have been active in the West Bank and Gaza, either in delivering budget support, conducting projects, or providing technical assistance for PFM reform. Among the donors supporting the PFM reform agenda, the World Bank prepared a number of analytical reports, including a Public Expenditure Review (PER) that was released in 2007; a Country Financial Accountability Assessment (CFAA); and a Country Procurement Assessment Report (CPAR) in 2004. The International Monetary Fund (IMF) provided strategic advice on both budget execution and budget preparation reforms following the formation of the Caretaker Government in 2007. The United

Kingdom's Department for International Development (DFID) has conducted projects supporting the preparation of a development plan (the PRDP) and improving budget preparation. The European Union (EU) has taken a specific interest in the areas of internal and external audit, and the United States Agency for International Development USAID has supported projects aimed at general capacity building.

Substantive Reform Agenda

An informal Public Expenditure Financial Accountability (PEFA) assessment was completed alongside the 2007 PER. The following sections set out the reform agenda in each of the six sections of the PEFA. A summary of the PEFA indicator scores is in the annex to this chapter. Using a four-point rating scale, the assessment produces the results shown in table 13.1.

Table 13.1. West Bank and Gaza Abbreviated Summary of PEFA Indicator Scores

PEFA Score	Number of Indicators
A (best)	0
B	4
C	11
D (worst)	12
Not Rated	4[a]
Total	31[b]

Source: World Bank.
Note: a. Includes the 3 tax administration indicators that form part of the PEFA framework.
b. PEFA comprises 28 system indicators and 3 donor indicators.

Credibility of the Budget. When considered on a commitment basis, the aggregate recurrent budget is a realistic indication of likely expenditures. Because reallocations during budget execution remain a common practice, there can be significant variances within the expenditure categories. In addition, while considerable effort has been made to clear past arrears, liquidity constraints created by inconsistent donor flows mean that it is common to find a buildup of expenditure arrears, as there is not a commitment control system in place.

One of the major reforms that improved the realism of the recurrent budget is the introduction of controls on the wage bill. This has addressed an earlier problem where civil and security recruitment was not in line with the provisions in the budget.

The development budget is almost entirely financed through donor projects. The timing of these projects is beyond the direct control of the PA, and the budget is regularly substantially under executed.

Comprehensiveness and Transparency. A range of reforms have been introduced to improve the transparency of the PFM system. Following reforms in 2002, the PA's banking arrangements are managed through a central treasury account at a commercial bank.[2] Prior to the reform, line ministries had separate bank accounts from which they received revenue and made expenditures. The reform consolidated PA revenue flows and cash balances, although donor funds are generally separate. Changes are now being introduced to consolidate the small cash balances held for budget execution by line ministries.

A range of improvements have been made to the transparency of the budget with the publication of a budget book. This includes information on macroeconomic assumptions, the deficit, and how it will be financed, among other information.

In order to improve the transparency with which state assets are managed, the PIF began operating as an independent investment company from 2003 onwards. Its chief objective is to safeguard and consolidate the Palestinian people's investments and property, both in West Bank and Gaza and abroad. Management of the Petroleum Commission, the PA's petroleum monopoly, was taken over directly by MOF. A number of monopoly arrangements were reformed and the companies were sold by the PIF. The Cement Company is the only remaining monopoly within the PIF portfolio. Prior to the PIF there was limited transparency in the functioning and financing of state enterprises.

A system of monthly reporting through the MOF website was introduced in 2002. While the procedure stopped operating during the period of the Hamas government (in part because the expenditure process was fragmented and necessary information was not available to the MOF), it was reintroduced by the Caretaker Government in 2008.

One area where reform continues to be necessary is budget classification. A different classification is used for budgeting than for accounting, and neither classification is aligned with the *Government Finance Statistics Manual* (GFSM) 2001. There is a proposal to unify the classifications using a revised budget classification for the 2011 Budget.

Policy-Based Budgeting. As indicated earlier, the reforms introduced by the Minister of Finance Salam Fayyad from 2002 initially focused on expenditure control and oversight. Relatively less attention was given to enhancing the policy focus of the budget. This is reflected in the PEFA, which identified a number of significant weaknesses in the procedures for budget preparation. However, a range of reforms initiated since 2007 (and supported by a DFID project) have substantially improved the situation. The MOF and the MOP had tended to work independently when preparing the recurrent and development budgets, but for the 2009 budget sectoral teams of MOF and MOP staff worked together—although the MOP staff generally had the lead. Budget submissions from line ministries were required to be based on a strategy for each ministry and to have a medium term focus. An effort was made to identify the recurrent expenditures associated with possible investment projects at the time they are being considered. For 2009, the information had a minimal impact on budget decision allocations, but it is expected to become more relevant over time.

For the 2009 budget, the line ministries were also asked to present a combined recurrent and development budget based on a program structure. The aim of the budget reforms is to eventually introduce program budgeting. The reform was mainly led by the MOP and the definition of programs was largely left to each ministry to decide. This has resulted in a range of different approaches being adopted. In time, the programs will need to be revised and standardized. In order for expenditure against the programs to be monitored in budget execution, some of the programs will also need to be simplified. The accounting system will not be able to manage the complex cost allocations that were adopted by some ministries.

The IMF recently provided advice on priority reforms for budget preparation. While commending the reforms to date, they cautioned against trying to move too quickly on the program budgeting reforms. The mission also recommended measures to improve the transparency and accountability of the development budget. The development budget continues to be mainly financed by donors and much of the aggregated expenditure presented in the budget is outside the control of the MOF.

Predictability and Control in Budget Execution. A number of reforms are taking place to improve controls during budget execution. A cash plan to assist in managing budget execution was prepared for the first time for the 2009 budget. While this addresses one of the weaknesses identified in the PEFA assessment, cash management continues to be complicated by the unpredictability of donor flows that finance about half of the recurrent budget. As a result, an important use of the cash plan will be to communicate the PA's cash needs to donors. A Debt Management Department was established by the MOF in Ramallah in 2008 to replace the department that earlier operated in Gaza. One of the first tasks of the unit is to recreate the external debt records that were lost during the Gaza conflict in early 2009.

Payroll controls have improved substantially in 2007 and 2008. They now provide more assurance on the integrity of an item that in the original 2009 budget constitutes more than 50 percent of recurrent expenditure. In particular, the payroll system is now connected with the accounting system of the MOF; security forces are now integrated with the civilian payroll; a separation of duties has been implemented between the payroll and IT department; and a separate financial controllers department reviews the payroll on a monthly basis.

A draft procurement law has been developed with the support of the World Bank. The law aims to improve on the earlier law that was both incomplete and insufficiently robust to provide for a clear, rules-based environment for conducting public procurement. The reforms associated with the new law include: (1) establishing an independent public procurement agency under the new procurement law; (2) preparing standard bidding documents based on the new law; and (3) preparing a user's manual and guidelines.

A new Internal Audit Department was established in 2004. Support for the unit has been provided through an EU project. While the PEFA assessment recognized that good initial progress was made by the department, it was understood that it would take time for it to be fully functional.

Controls over expenditure were strengthened by creating a separate Department of Financial Control in 2004. MOF financial controllers were out-posted to spending ministries, and they report to the Director-General of the Financial Control. This system replaced the previous system, in which each ministry had a financial controller reporting to its minister. Recently, the management of the financial controllers has been brought under the Accountant General.

The lack of commitment controls is a weakness identified in the PEFA. With the introduction of the new accounting system, commitment controls were intended to be introduced during 2009 but are not yet in place.

Accounting, Recording, and Reporting. From mid-2007 on, the accounting system based in Gaza was not available to the PA in Ramallah. A new computerized accounting system was developed by customizing a system operating earlier in the Ministry of Education. This system was able to start processing payments in the MOF from January 2008—only four months after the project started—but because it is a bespoke system it has continued to be further refined and developed. A particular focus has been on addressing the findings of a review by Ernst and Young, which identified a number of weaknesses, especially in the security of the system.[3] During 2009, the system has been progressively rolled out to line ministries.

With the operation of the new accounting system, the release of monthly budget reports was reintroduced by the 15th of the following month in early 2008. These reports are posted on the MOF website. In addition, the MOF has been able to prepare financial statements for 2008 and these are to be audited by the State Audit and Administrative Control Bureau (SAACB). This would be the first audit of financial statements since the 2003 accounts. The earlier audit was heavily qualified. Because the SAACB is being supported by the Office of the Auditor General of Norway it has some credibility, and the MOF has been committed to improving the quality of the accounts it presents.

DFID is supporting the MOF in preparing the financial statements for audit and the World Bank has provided strategic advice. Through this support, a range of improvements to accounting procedures have been identified. These will be the focus of the substantive reform agenda during 2009 and 2010. The work will include specifying accounting standards that, to date, have not been disclosed.

External Scrutiny and Audit. The SAACB was established in 2005 but had few staff until a major recruitment took place in early 2008. The SAACB's mandate includes the audit of almost 10,000 institutions at the levels of central government, local government, and nongovernmental organizations (NGOs), but to date it has not had the capacity for this task. A range of donors have recently started working with the SAACB. An EU project is designed to build capacity in the SAACB, and a needs assessment was carried out in late 2008. The project is expected to start in 2010.

In 2009, the SAACB is expected to complete an audit of the financial statements of the PA. As mentioned earlier, to support this activity the Office of the Auditor General of Norway is providing technical guidance and has already conducted a series of training seminars.

The SAACB is a member of Arab Organization of Supreme Audit Institutions (ARABOSAI) and Asian Organization of Supreme Audit Institutions (ASOSAI), and is working towards becoming a member of the International Organization of Supreme Audit Institutions (INTOSAI). Furthermore, it has been working on developing close bilateral relationships and has signed two bilateral agreements with Jordan and Kuwait that provide for assistance with training staff.

The Parliament (PLC) has not been sitting since a number of members were arrested in 2006. The PEFA indicates that the Budget Committee of the Parliament was active but lacked the information and resources to adequately fulfill its mandate.

Summary of the Substantive Reform Agenda. Since 2007, there has been an extremely large reform agenda touching on almost all aspects of the PFM system. Some of these efforts are independent, such as reforms in the SAACB. But there are two large components of work—one on budget preparation and the other on budget execution—where a number of different reforms are connected. Many of the reforms are still work in progress, and for this reason it is too early to judge the final outcome. But the indications are generally positive—although the budget reforms are moving more slowly than the MOP and the MOF had hoped. It does not appear that the size of the reform agenda alone is a problem in West Bank and Gaza.

While many of the reforms carried out since 2002 have made a significant contribution to improved PFM, a number stand out as particularly impressive successes:

- The creation of the central treasury account has improved the control of cash balances by the PA—and after a period of fragmentation during the Hamas government—was quickly reestablished by the Caretaker Government in 2007.
- The establishment of the Palestinian Investment Fund (PIF) has substantially improved the oversight of the state assets and successfully reduced the potential for abuse. The PIF is considered to be a transparent and well run organization, and the legislative arrangements for the Fund should ensure it is enduring.
- The introduction of monthly reporting on budget execution has improved fiscal transparency. The system stopped operating during the Hamas government but was quickly reintroduced by the Caretaker Government.
- The quick implementation of a new accounting system in 2007 and early 2008 was particularly impressive. Because of the crisis faced by the PA, the process followed in developing the system was not ideal. But the fact that it was able to process payments within four months of the concept being discussed was exceptional. The system has required further development since that time, and the ongoing costs of managing a bespoke system may be problematic.

In contrast, a major failure was an IT project that the EU carried out for revenue administration. The project was abandoned by the PA after €5 million was spent.

Implementation Strategies for Reform

There has been no grand strategy to guide the PFM reform process, although a number of recent donor reports have strongly advised that a reform action plan be developed. In the initial 2002–05 period, Minister of Finance Salam Fayyad deliberately took an "opportunistic" approach to pushing reform priorities guided by a few basic principles. The approach, which has continued since mid-2007, was outlined as follows in a recent study of the PFM reforms in the West Bank and Gaza.[4]

Focusing on the Structural. Minister Fayyad wanted to tackle the structural aspects of the PFM system instead of focusing on corruption directly. He explains, "When you get into a situation like this, people are usually looking at the 'sexier' aspects of managing the public finance question, corruption, who took what, when and how—but not this structural aspect. I was really preoccupied with that. It's not that there is no corruption or anything like that—but I felt it necessary, and we took the approach that was based on, 'Let's stop the leakage. Let's stop the leak and make sure the system functions well here on out.' Then we go back to the extent that there were infractions and all that—we can deal with that—but to look back doesn't have much effect."[5]

Knowing the Priorities. Fayyad began by focusing on the major structural problems related to revenue and expenditure management and the budget. He observes, "There are elements without which you cannot have a well functioning public finance system. Conceptually, unless you have central treasury operation, unless you have consolidation of your revenues, and unless you are executing expenditures within a budgetary framework, you do not have much of a public finance system to speak of. You can be talking about catching somebody stealing some money here and there, but that doesn't do it. Whatever it is you do, that has to be the key objective of policy early on."

Being Opportunistic. At the same time, Minister Fayyad adopted a flexible view, recognizing that he could not determine a priori the sequencing of reforms or expect to have control over the entire process. He explains, "The context in which you are operating has to be kept in mind all the time. It's not easy. You are working within a system of deeply entrenched habits—not good ones—so you basically have one of two choices. Either to come in and say, "This is what I want to do. Either it's done, or I'm out"—which is what everyone was expecting, or maybe even banking on. Or, you could be opportunistic: do what you can, as soon as you can do it, wherever you can do it. I chose the latter way.... But, at all times have clarity as to what is important and what is not too important."[6] He describes his approach as "patient, deliberate, methodical, and opportunistic, looking for an opening here and there."

Generating Credibility from the Start. Minister Fayyad wanted to generate confidence in the reform agenda by taking specific, quick steps that made an impression. He explains, "I have learned about the need to move fast, and make an impression. It gets more difficult with time, not easier. You need to use your success as a stepping stone. Success breeds success. If you say 'give me time, I will assess,' that is wrong approach. You need to immediately begin to make an impression."

In the period from mid-2007 the approach continued to be flexible and the focus shifted in response to emerging problems. For example, payments systems and banking arrangements were the priority in 2007. With the preparation of financial statements, the weaknesses in accounting procedures have become more important.

Other Implementation Issues. The management of the reforms varies significantly from initiative to initiative. The reforms in MOF have not followed project management systems. For example, the main driver of the reforms that started in mid-2007 was the Accountant General, and he managed the reform process with limited interaction with others in the MOF. This avoided bureaucratic delays and established a strong sense of ownership by the Accountant General, but it created tension within the MOF as other managers and staff felt excluded from the process. It also meant that linkages between the reforms and other work of the MOF were not always made, and that some important areas were given low priority. However, with the donor supported projects, such as the reforms in budget preparation project in the MOP, there have been formal reporting arrangements and a structured approach to project management.

While many issues are decided by the Minister of Finance, senior civil service managers are prepared to take decisions. There are solid technical decision makers in the MOF, but the human resource capacity is thin. The lack of depth in the MOF has placed a heavy burden on key managers and the success of the reforms can be directly attributed to the skills of these managers.

Specific financial incentives were not provided to support the reforms. Study tours were used occasionally as opportunities to broaden the understanding of staff, but these were only for a small number. More importantly, some civil servants were motivated through non-financial rewards. For example in relaunching the monthly reporting process in 2008, the PM made a strong endorsement of the importance of the documents and gave a personal commitment that the reports would be posted by the 15th of the following month. This was a strong motivation for the staff preparing the reports—who subsequently worked weekends and public holidays to ensure that the reports were posted in time. There is also a strong sense of nationalism driving many of the reformers, who were working in an environment where the lack of effective institutions is an argument used by some against establishing a Palestinian state.

While there are examples of the use of pilots during the reform process, this has not been the norm. Instead, many of the changes were introduced across the board—recognizing that the initial performance would be deficient, but that it would improve over time. Examples include reforms to the budget preparation system, and the changes to financial regulations which were applied to all agencies.

The self-reinforcing nature of some of the reforms has been an important attribute. Good examples are the reforms to the payment processes, payroll procedures, and monthly reporting. Once introduced, these procedures have continued. Even when there was a break in monthly reporting during the Hamas period, it was reinitiated without too much difficulty. In contrast, sectoral analysis is in the early stages of development as part of the budget reforms, but it is already clear that this will be a more difficult reform to sustain through time.

Donors have monitored the progress of some reforms through frequent missions by technical teams. In addition, the World Bank has an advisor working closely with the MOF on a day to day basis, and DFID has a team embedded within the MOP. A donor coordination system helps to keep donor representatives informed of progress. The Fiscal Sector Working Group is one of the committees established through this system, and it has been used to ensure that the donor community is informed of progress with reforms. However, until recently, PFM issues have been given lower priority to fiscal discussions at these meetings.

Political Economy of Reform

Over the course of the past decade, there has been little political stability and this, coupled with the associated fiscal crises, has created a challenging reform environment. Externally, there have been distractions created by the difficult relationship with Israel and the inconsistent budget support flows from the international community. Internally, the differences between the President and Prime Minister in 2003, along with the political break between Hamas and Fatah and the bifurcation of PA administrative structures between the West Bank and Gaza, have been particularly disruptive. The MOF has been unable to operate in Gaza from mid-2007 on and has needed to replicate many functions and systems again in the West Bank. Although the separation of Gaza created a new set of challenges, the period since mid-2007 has generally been a stable period for reform under the technocratic Caretaker Government.

A positive aspect of the political challenges is that it created opportunities for reform. In some areas, there was a complete failure of earlier systems. The crisis provided an opportunity to make improvements when developing new replacements. Moreover, the disruptions meant that there was a tolerance for problems and hence a willingness to introduce new approaches, while knowing that initial implementation would not be perfect. A related issue is that the PA is a relatively new institution, and the old procedures had not become entrenched.

Another strong positive of the political environment is that Salam Fayyad has had extended terms as Minister of Finance since 2002 (excluding the period of elections and Hamas control), and this has provided continuity in leadership of the MOF. There has also been continuity in many of the key positions within the MOF. Reforms have progressed furthest when there has been a combination of strategic support from the Minister of Finance and technical support within the MOF. The staff in the MOF have not changed significantly and they have also been supportive of reforms. In particular, the Accountant General has been a key driver of the accounting reforms that have taken place since mid-2007.

In the initial 2002–05 period, the reform process was highly politicized. Reforms were identified with one faction in the internal political debate. There was also a general concern that the reforms were removing some of the earlier discretion of expenditure that supported the patronage based system. For example, the development of the PIF created more transparency in the operation of state companies.

There have also been problems where the management of a reform spanned two agencies. Both the MOP and the MOF have a stake in the budget preparation reforms, but MOF lost capacity with the closure of the Gaza office. As donor support was primarily linked to MOP, it had a stronger role. MOF also has a stronger focus on compliance and payment issues than the policy and planning elements of budgeting. This in part reflects the interest of the Minister. The lack of an agreed vision for the budget reform has created problems and these continue.

A further major drive has come from the donor community. With the PA needing substantial support for the recurrent budget, the donors have been pushing for PFM reforms that would give them comfort in disbursing budget support to the PA. Donor support has also been a driver for the Preparation of a Development Plan (PRDP) and program budgeting initiatives, as donors are looking for more information on how the budget support is being used. The West Bank and Gaza does not have an IMF program, but donor engagement has been established through a trust fund operated by the World Bank. The policy benchmarks set out in the trust fund have in general been viewed positively by the reformers as a way to strengthen their hand in internal debates, and not as a mechanism to impose reforms on the economy. For this reason, the Minister of Finance pushed for a new World Bank trust fund during 2008 even though the commitments of unconditional budget support suggested that this was not necessary. This approach has its limitations, however, as was demonstrated in late 2005 when the PA failed to follow the conditions on controlling the wage bill.

On technical issues, perhaps the most important donor contribution has been in providing strategic advice on the PFM system, which has helped to shape the reform agenda. This has been particularly important for the MOF, where the Minister of Finance has not been enthusiastic about having international experts based in the ministry. His view is that this can result in the expert doing the work and not building the capacity in the MOF staff. The MOF has therefore relied on the recommendations from short missions. This approach has been successful, but is being revised as more complicated reforms are addressed. For example, in preparing the 2008 accounts more intensive guidance (involving an international expert) was needed and this is likely to also be necessary as the accounting procedures are updated. A priority in this work is to ensure that the international expert also develops the capacity of MOF staff. With the MOP and the proposed support for the SAACB, donors will work through resident experts and consultants.

Key Conclusions

The case of the West Bank and Gaza is an example that substantial reform agendas are possible provided there is the support at both the political and technical levels. In this case, the Minister of Finance and the MOF have had a common vision for the changes and have been committed to reform, especially in payment processing and bank consolidation areas. The more limited success of budget reforms can be attributed to the split management between MOP and MOF, and the fact that the Minister of Finance gave priority to reforms aimed at expenditure control and put less emphasis on the links between planning and budgeting.

Both the Minister of Finance and the key MOF staff have preferred informal management systems and a reform plan was not developed. This reduced bureaucratic delays, but it meant that the need for some important reforms, such as those required in the accounting area, were not being realized and initiated as early as they should have been.

The role of donors has been especially useful in providing strategic guidance and in strengthening the hand of the reformers in internal debates by linking support to the reform agenda. Although the internal and external political environment has been extremely challenging, this has also had a positive element by encouraging a willingness on the part of the PA reformers to adopt change. The willingness to change existing systems can also be attributed to the PA being a young institution without deeply established systems that are resistant to reform.

Some of the features of the West Bank and Gaza—such as the political challenges—are unique. But the lessons in the role of leadership and management of the reform process are applicable to other economies.

Annex: West Bank and Gaza PEFA Assessment

Table 13A.1. Overview of the Performance Indicator Set

Indicator	MENA Regional PEFA Study 2010	Grade
Credibility of the budget	Aggregate expenditure out-turn compared to original approved budget	B
	Composition of expenditure out-turn compared to original approved budget	C
	Aggregate revenue out-turn compared to original approved budget	B
	Stock and monitoring of expenditure payment arrears	D+
Comprehensiveness and transparency	Classification of the budget	D
	Comprehensiveness of information included in budget documentation	B
	Extent of unreported government operations	C+
	Transparency of intergovernmental fiscal relations	D+
	Oversight of aggregate fiscal risk from other public sector entities	D+
	Public access to key fiscal information	C
Policy-based budgeting	Orderliness and participation in the annual budget process	C+
	Multiyear perspective in fiscal planning, expenditure policy, and budgeting	D
Predictability and control in budget execution	Transparency of taxpayer obligations and liabilities	Not Rated
	Effectiveness of measures for taxpayer registration and tax assessment	Not Rated
	Effectiveness in collection of tax payments	Not Rated
	Predictability in the availability of funds for commitment of expenditures	D+
	Recording and management of cash balances, debt, and guarantees	C
	Effectiveness of payroll controls	C+
	Competition, value for money, and controls in procurement	Not Rated
	Effectiveness of internal controls for nonsalary expenditure	D+
	Effectiveness of internal audit	C
Accounting, recording, and reporting	Timeliness and regularity of accounts reconciliation	C
	Availability of information on resources received by service delivery units	D
	Quality and timeliness of in-year budget reports	B
	Quality and timeliness of annual financial statements	D+
External scrutiny and audit	Scope, nature, and follow-up of external audit	D
	Legislative scrutiny of the annual budget law	C+
	Legislative scrutiny of external audit reports	D
Donor practices	Predictability of direct budget support	D
	Financial information provided by donors for budgeting and reporting on project and program aid	C
	Proportion of aid that is managed by use of national procedures	C

Source: World Bank.

Notes

1. The agreement limited PA's role in a number of important dimensions where control remained with Israel. This included management of the borders and the associated fiscal revenues.

2. The PA does not have a Central Bank. In view of problems experienced with the freezing of bank balances at the central treasury account during the period of the Hamas government, the PA now operates its central account from two commercial banks.

3. Ernst and Young/Ministry of Finance, Palestine, *Systems Functionality Review Report*, 2008. This review was commissioned by the Ministry of Finance to provide them with assurance on the integrity of the new system.

4. Nagarajan, *Reforms to Public Financial Management in Palestine*, 2008.

5. Fayyad, Transcript, 2008.

6. Ibid.

CHAPTER 14

The Republic of Yemen

Arun Arya

General Overview

The Republic of Yemen is the poorest economy in the MENA region and faces daunting challenges in an uncertain global and regional environment. Significant progress has been made over the last few years, but living conditions for most of the 22 million Yemenis remain difficult. The Republic of Yemen's governance structures are complex and it remains an economy afflicted by security issues. The Republic of Yemen is unlikely to reach most Millennium Development Goals (MDGs) by 2015, and the situation is particularly dire for women. The Government is implementing a program of economic and governance reforms, but time is of the essence as oil resources are rapidly depleting while the population continues to grow at a rapid pace. The Republic of Yemen is also now beginning to be affected by the global economic crisis in spite of the financial sector's relative insulation.

The Republic of Yemen is a democratic state based on a multiparty parliamentary system. The executive branch is comprised of the President and the Council of Ministers, with executive authority established in the Office of the President and the Prime Minister being responsible for the day to day running of government affairs. The Minister of Finance is responsible for the management of public finances and appoints Accounting Officers to each ministry and department with responsibility for safeguarding of public funds; ensuring the application of funds as intended by parliament and in accordance with approved policy; maintaining financial records in accordance with the financial regulations; maintaining an efficient system of internal controls; and submitting the financial, accounting and stores records to the Central Organization of Control and Audit (COCA).

The parliament votes on the budget but has no authority to directly amend budget lines. The Ministry of Planning is responsible for the preparation of the investment budget. COCA is responsible for conducting external audit and special investigations for the Cabinet, the Minister of Finance, and the Public Accounts Committee. The Supreme Tender Committee is responsible for the endorsement of tenders over given thresholds. Line ministries are responsible for preparing and implementing their respective budgets. The Accounting Officers posted under each line ministry serve as the custodian of public funds for those ministries and the finance officers, accounts officers, cashiers, and procurement officers report administratively to the Accounting Officer of the line ministry in which they serve.

There are two main tiers of subnational government in the Republic of Yemen. The first is at the governorate level (22), whose executive is headed by a governor. There is a local council whose members are elected by districts. The second tier are made up of the district councils (303) headed by a council chairman. Both tiers have the right to raise revenues.

The economy is heavily aid-dependent, and a major part of the Public Investment Program is financed by donors. The government expects donors to finance around US$1.6 billion in 2009 and 2010 respectively, which is about 50 percent of its total Public Investment Program of US$3.3 billion during those years. Among the Republic of Yemen's various development partners, the core group supporting public financial management (PFM) reform is comprised of the UK Department for International Development (DFID), the Netherlands, the United Nations Development Programme (UNDP), and the World Bank. Other donors working on PFM reforms outside this core group include the United States Agency for International Development (USAID), and the German development agency GTZ.

Substantive Reform Agenda

A Public Expenditure and Financial Accountability (PEFA) assessment was carried out by the World Bank in 2007, with a particular focus on the period from FY 2004–06. The Ministry of Finance was deeply involved in this assessment. It constituted a PEFA Task Force to review the draft PEFA report and give its recommendations to the PEFA Secretariat, and the report was finalized in June 2008. A summary of the PEFA indicator scores is in the annex to this chapter. Using a four-point rating scale, the assessment produces the results shown in table 14.1. The government accepts the PEFA Assessment and has placed it on its official website for public use. It is also using the assessment as an input into the next phase of its PFM reforms.

Table 14.1. The Republic of Yemen Abbreviated Summary of PEFA Indicator Scores

PEFA Score	Number of Indicators
A (best)	5
B	7
C	6
D (worst)	9
Not Rated	4[a]
Total	31[b]

Source: World Bank.
Note: a. Includes the 3 donor indicators that form part of the PEFA framework.
b. PEFA comprises 28 system indicators and 3 donor indicators.

Credibility of the Budget. Approximately 75 percent of Government revenues derive from oil production.[1] Given this dependence and the price volatility of oil, the Government has adopted a conservative approach to revenue estimates to shield the budget from sharp revenue swings. As a result, the actual revenue out-turns tend to surpass budget projections. In principle, robust revenue achievements provide a sound starting point for achieving a credible budget. This policy posture on the revenue projections, however, has not been coupled with a fiscal policy that specifies how any excess revenues will be managed. In practice, much of the surplus has been directed to primary recurrent expenditure, thus undermining budget credibility on the expenditure side. In addition, the current policy of subsidizing domestic petroleum consumption means that, with increasing oil prices and the subsequent increase in government revenues, subsidy payments automatically increase. However, an analysis of the increased expenditures shows that even when domestic petroleum subsidies are excluded, the increase of expenditure over original budget estimates is still substantial and to a degree that undermines the credibility of the budget.

In addition to weaknesses in budget preparation, the poor matching of aggregate expenditure out-turn figures to the budget estimates reflect a range of weaknesses in the process of budget execution. There is a lack of predictability in budget releases; weak cash management; uneven commitment controls; less than fully effective salary expenditure controls; and a practice of ex post approval of the supplementary budget by parliament.

The budget process occurs within a pre-announced resource envelope based upon fiscal forecasts and taking into account policy considerations. However, this top down framework is not linked to the detailed budget preparation of line ministries. The Republic of Yemen is taking the first steps towards implementing a multiyear framework for budget estimates but this process still needs, as a pre-requisite, to develop stronger links between the fiscal framework and the sector development plans. The PFM systems are capable of delivering predictable and well controlled virement procedures. However, there are considerable adjustments made above the level of line ministries to budget appropriations, and this practice tends to undermine the credibility of the budget.

No monitoring of arrears is undertaken, so the arrears cannot be quantified. There is also no reliable data maintained on the level of arrears from the past two years. While the first four PEFA indicators (PI-1 to PI-4) focus upon the recurrent expenditure, the issue of the credibility of the budget must take into account the whole budget, including that portion which is financed by international loans and grants (see indicators PI-7 and D-2). The lack of reliable information on donor funded budget estimates has resulted in the Ministry of Planning largely guessing what such investment is likely to be. As a result, the Ministry of Planning has tended to adopt an extremely conservative posture, which has sometimes led to projects being left out of the budget estimates. These practices tend to undermine the credibility of the budget.

Comprehensiveness and Transparency. In the Republic of Yemen the extent of budget documentation is voluminous, with 38 separate volumes presented to parliament. This includes a macro-fiscal policy statement, as well as details on expenditure and revenues for special funds and local authorities in addition to the line ministries. The budget at the time of PEFA Assessment adopted an economic and administrative classification, although it has since been revised to also include a functional structure based upon the United Nation's Classification of the Functions of Government (COFOG) standard. Fiscal forecasts are realistic although not always adequately integrated into the budget process. There are effective debt management controls, with the Minister of Planning and International Cooperation being the sole authority for entering into loan agreements. All loans also require the Minister of Finance's endorsement and the parliament's ratification.

The Central Bank of Yemen (CBY) operates a Treasury Single Account with regular reconciliation of all transactions. To achieve full effectiveness, the Treasury Single Account would require closer management by the Ministry of Finance. There are some extra-budgetary operations financed out of internally generated funds held in special accounts by some of the line ministries, though these are not a significant ratio of total expenditure. All revenues collected directly by line ministries and revenue agencies, including the Oil Ministry, are transferred to the Consolidated Fund. All expenditure is made through a centralized payments system. While the majority of donor funds are deposited in the CBY, there are a number of major donors who do not adhere to this arrangement, so the tracking of project implementation is less regular or timely.

The recurrent expenditure allocations to local authorities are managed in the same way as the allocations to line ministries. There has been significant reform in recent years with respect to the local authorities. The Local Authorities Law (2001) provides for a rule based horizontal allocation of central government disbursements. However, without effective monitoring and evaluation mechanisms, the rule based allocation of resources has only been partially put into effect.

The transparency of budget management has improved in recent years. In particular, there have been significant improvements with respect to the amount of budgetary and fiscal information that is being placed on Government websites. However, public access to budget and other fiscal documentation at Government bookshops, libraries and other physical outlets is lacking.

Policy-Based Budgeting. The first steps towards implementing a multiyear budgetary framework have been taken. The GoY has issued a medium-term national development framework (DPPR) that clearly states the medium term policy objectives. It was developed within a macro-fiscal framework (though not fully costed) and includes recurrent cost implications. A macro-fiscal analysis is performed each year (but without sectoral work being undertaken) before budget preparation begins. However the analysis is not linked to the process of budget preparation. Debt sustainability analysis is regularly undertaken and the debt stock is monitored and reconciled on a regular basis. Forecasts of fiscal aggregates on the basis of economic classifications are prepared for three years on a rolling basis. Statements of sector strategies exist for just a few sectors. These are not all fully costed, and where costings are prepared they are not in line with the aggregate fiscal forecasts.

The budget cycle is well defined and the call circular issues clear guidelines that provide a sound context for the budget process. The budget process encompasses policy input both at the beginning through cabinet approved sector ceilings, as well as at the end by way of parliamentary debate. The executive completes its budget submissions prior to the start of the fiscal year after allowing for two and half months of budget preparation by the line ministries and a full negotiation process. The Parliament approves the appropriations before the start of the fiscal year after subjecting the budget proposals to debate over a two month period. The budget documents are detailed and address many of the requirements for both meaningful budgetary oversight and to properly guide implementation. However, the parliamentary recommendations are not incorporated into the budget in a transparent manner. While a written parliamentary recommendation is included in the appropriations law, along with an undertaking to implement such recommendations signed by the Minister of Finance, there would be greater transparency if an approved budget reflecting the parliamentary recommendations was also included in the budget documents.

Predictability and Control in Budget Execution. There are three main sources for domestic revenue in the Republic of Yemen: (1) oil revenues arising through royalties, income tax and government shares of production; (2) income taxes, both company and individual; and (3) customs revenues. The oil revenues are governed by Production Share Agreements (PSAs) entered into with 12 oil producing companies. While daily payment of tax receipts into the Consolidated Revenue Fund along with regular reconciliations are carried out by the Tax Agencies, reconciliations by the Oil Ministry are not performed regularly. There are significant tax arrears, dominated by a large uncollectible component which the authorities are considering writing off. The collection ratio of tax arrears remains low.

The adoption of a six-month general warrant for the authority to incur recurrent expenditure, as well as the three-month general warrant for capital expenditure, should provide the basis for predictability in budget execution. Unfortunately, at present, the warrants are not based on a projection of cash flows. The absence of effective cash management leads to higher financing costs as the government is forced to make greater use of short term borrowings. The problem is further compounded by the practice of adjusting the general warrants during the period.

Virement control is strong. Virement control over transfers between budgetary chapters and sub-chapters are made at the level of the Ministry of Finance. The sub-account structure of the Treasury Single Account mirroring the chapter and sub-chapter ceilings facilitates effective virement control.

Since 2002, there has been a project to introduce an automated financial management system (AFMIS) in the MOF. The project has been significantly delayed, but AFMIS is currently being piloted in four ministries and will eventually be rolled out in others. It is hoped that its implementation will improve the level of budget execution control. However, while a commitment control module was expected to be built into AFMIS, this function is not yet integrated into the system. Manual commitment control systems are not uniformly implemented across all ministries. The weak commitment controls, along with the updates of the General Warrant ceilings, contribute to the overall lack of budget credibility.

The CBY is currently performing the treasury function, which in most economies is done by the MOF. The MOF is looking to take over this function and this reform is included under the PFM reform agenda. However, more than 80 percent of CBY's staff are engaged in the treasury function, and the MOF does not have the capacity to implement the function as of now. Although CBY does not object to the function being shifted to the MOF, it privately expresses concern about the future of its employees.

The Republic of Yemen, for the most part, uses a centralized payments system out of the Consolidated Fund held in the CBY and operated as a Treasury Single Account. The system facilitates daily bank balance consolidation that informs and controls payments. The lack of effective commitment controls however has led to liquidity shortages, which have delayed payments and contributed to what appears to be a high level of arrears — although, as noted above, there is no specific data on the size of arrears.

The Ministry of Local Administration (MOLA) recently championed some amendments to the Decentralization Act recently that paved the way for greater decentralization. It has also launched the Decentralization Strategy. If the decentralization strategy is be implemented in full, then the MOF will also have to decentralize its authority to the governorates. The MOF is concerned that the governorates do not have the capacity to take over this responsibility.

There has been substantial reform in the area of procurement by way of the passing of a new Tender Law in July 2007. This is an important first step towards improving the control of budget execution. The previous law did not establish an authority responsible for procurement policy and regulatory oversight, nor did it establish an independent procurement appeals mechanism. These have been addressed in the new law. USAID is supporting public procurement reforms in the Republic of Yemen and has provided training to government officials of pilot ministries on standard bidding documents. The National Procurement Manual is being prepared by the World Bank.

Despite the reform efforts, both COCA and the Chamber of Commerce paint a troubling picture of procurement practices in the Republic of Yemen. The picture presented is one rife with collusion and lack of competition. It includes the abuse of contract variations with subsequent project overruns, non-transparent tender evaluations, an excessive resort to direct procurement methods, and the use of "slicing" to bypass procurement and authorization thresholds.

The management of the payroll is another area where control appears to be less than satisfactory. A Civil Service Modernization Project was started in 1998, which aimed to establish a clean personnel database by 2001. The project was restarted in 2005 with a clean up exercise (principally of double dippers and ghost workers) through a new database that includes biometric control data. The clean up exercise covers approximately 50 percent of Government employees. It does not include a significant portion of the Ministry of Defense. Progress to date on the biometric system has not been coupled with direct database links between the cleaned personnel database and the payroll. There are still less than adequate reconciliation controls for the addition, termination, and modification of personnel records in the fragmented payroll files. Until effective links are established between the personnel database and the payroll files, the payroll will be vulnerable to ghost workers and double dippers creeping back over time.

There are two main components of internal audit in the Republic of Yemen. The first, resident in all line ministries, limits its audit activities to operational audits. The Ministry of Finance also has an Internal Audit Unit with jurisdiction over all line ministries, local authorities, and public corporations. In addition to financial audits, this unit carries out limited systems and value for money audits. They prepare an annual work plans using a risk based approach to identify areas of focus and report regularly to the Minister of Finance and relevant line minister on their findings, with copies of reports submitted to COCA and the Cabinet. However, with a full time professional staff of only 16, their effectiveness is limited. There is also only limited follow up on the audit findings of the Internal Audit. The head of the public entity is accountable for the management of public funds. There is a Follow-Up Department within the MOF responsible for implementing corrective measures and audit recommendations. Finally, within the Finance Offices of each line ministry are Inspectors and Controllers. Their primary role is quality assurance of expenditure procedures through the application of pre-audit methods.

Accounting, Recording, and Reporting. Government accounting standards are applied across all ministries consistently. While the appropriations accounts adopt a few of the mandatory standards of IPSAS (such as comparison between budget and actual, the inclusion of financial assets and liabilities, and the details of revenues and expenditure), not all of the mandatory standards are met. The CBY submits monthly budget Release Reports to the MOF based upon payments made—although these are highly aggregated. The line ministries submit Monthly Budget Execution Returns. However, these are submitted on average 12 weeks after the close of the period. They do not distinguish between commitments and expenditure. However, they do distinguish advances and payments and allow direct comparison of budget implementation to the original budget. The reporting format allows line ministries to report on accrued arrears, but this is often not followed. The line ministry reports are consolidated by the MOF, but with the delays their effectiveness as a management tool is undermined.

The Final Accounts Directorate of the MOF consolidates the accounts prepared by the line ministries and prepares annual statements with a table of financial assets and liabilities as well as revenue and expenditure information. The accounts are typically completed within nine months of the end of the fiscal year, but outside of the six month requirement of the Finance Law. One of the challenges in preparing the accounts is obtaining complete or timely financial expenditure data from donors on the project expenditures they execute directly.

There have been assessments on the level of expenditure carried out at the level of front-line facilities in the past three years, including a Public Expenditure Tracking Survey in the Ministry of Education which was supported by the World Bank, a Public Expenditure Review covering Health carried out by USAID, and a Public Expenditure Tracking Survey in the Ministry of Health with support from DFID. These pointed to difficulties with salary payments and weak bottom up budget preparation procedures leading to a misalignment of resources.

External Scrutiny and Audit. the Republic of Yemen is characterized by a well structured parliamentary oversight of the government's budget estimates. The approval process includes a debate on fiscal policy in addition to reviewing the details of the revenue and expenditure estimates. The Parliament was less involved in reviewing actual expenditures, but it has made a thorough review of the 2007 accounts, preparing a three volume 350 page review of the audit findings that included interviewing a number of Government officials responsible for the audit findings.

The submission of the audit reports and audited financial statements from COCA is timely, and COCA follows up on the audit findings. However, COCA is concerned that it does not receive the final accounts from the MOF in time, leaving it very little time to conduct its audit. A second major issue relates to the independence of COCA, which among other things includes a demand from COCA that it be granted a "single line budget" and authority to report directly to the Parliament. COCA also sees the present internal audit system as an encroachment on its authority, as it is external rather than internal to the line ministries.

COCA has sought to adopt many INTOSAI standards, but this is probably best characterized as a work in progress. A draft audit bill has been completed and is currently under consideration by the President. It will address, among other things, the independence of the President of COCA as well as the organization. The German development agency GTZ is supporting COCA in its institutional restructuring and capacity building.

Implementation Strategies for Reform

The PFM reform program in the Republic of Yemen has followed a very formal process. The program was developed based on a number of studies carried out by the World Bank and the International Monetary Fund (IMF), including a *Country Financial and Accountability Assessment* (2004), and a *Country Procurement Assessment Report* (2003). In August 2005, Cabinet approved the Public Finance Management Reform Strategy and endorsed the components of General Budget Reform. A Public Finance Management Reform Action Plan was then formulated on the basis of above Strategy. It was divided into two phases, with the first phase to be implemented during 2006–08 (which was subsequently extended until June 2009). A Partnership Agreement was signed in May 2006 between Government and Donors to implement the PFM Reform Strategy. Following this, a Project Agreement titled *Implementation of Public Financial Management Reform Action Plan* was signed between UNDP and Government in September 2006 with an objective of supporting Ministry of Finance to implement PFM as per its action plan. The project cost of US$3.6 million was shared by DFID, the Netherlands, and UNDP.

To implement the program, the Republic of Yemen has adopted an elaborate committee structure for managing its PFM reforms. The institutional arrangements for the PFM reform program vest overall responsibility for implementation with the Ministerial PFM Reform Committee, which meets annually and is responsible for the implementing the strategy and achieving the desired reform outcomes. The Committee is made up of the Minister and Vice Minister of Finance, the Minister of Planning, the Minister for Civil Service, the Minister for Local Authorities and the Governor of the Central Bank. A PFM Reform Task Force headed by the Deputy Minister of Finance in Charge of Budget has been set up, which is responsible for overseeing the implementation of the reforms. There are a number of technical committees that have been given responsibility for specific agendas and tasks.[2]

Notably, the AFMIS project is not linked to the PFM Reform Task Force, with the subsequent risk that the computerization effort will not reflect the requirements of the reformed PFM. The technical committees are supposed to report to the Follow-Up Committee on a quarterly basis, but in practice this does not happen. There is a separate AFMIS Task Force, but there is no representation from COCA or the Internal Audit Unit of the Ministry of Finance on the Task Force. This raises questions about whether AFMIS transaction and reporting controls are fully compliant with the PFM requirements. It also suggests that there is little coordination between the AFMIS Project and these audit institutions with respect to the development of effective audit techniques for auditing public finance management implemented on the AFMIS platform.

Responsibility for the implementation of various reform pillars is delegated to the relevant Accounting Officer in each ministry. While components have been defined for the technical committees, each is currently developing a matrix of activities, outputs, inputs, indicators and milestones. The PFM reform program has not been integrated as a separate program within the MOF budget. A large part of the reason for the absence of these important elements appears to be the rather severe capacity constraints. Having said that, the past few years have witnessed some progress in addressing the first element of sound PFM practice—the achievement of aggregate fiscal discipline. However, it should be noted that most of the reforms have centered upon MOF and Ministry of

Civil Service and Insurance activities rather than distributed actions rolled out to all the line ministries.

In the first phase, the Public Finance Management Reform Program was comprehensive and contained many elements of a sound PFM Reform program. However, it did not achieve its objectives. The program included a list of dated milestones, but it did not clearly distinguish activity start dates as well as end dates and whether pilot programs were to be employed or not. The project was managed by UNDP through a PFM Advisory Unit (PFMAU) located within the Finance Ministry. Problems arose from delays in setting up and staffing this PFMAU. A long-term international adviser was to head the PFMAU, but he arrived nine months after the project had been commissioned. There were also delays in the procurement of short-term consultants.

Such problems were compounded by the fact that roles and responsibilities at the government level were not clear. The project was to be implemented by the MOF, but some coordination was required with other agencies like COCA, the High Tender Board, the National Fiscal Training Institute (NFTI), the Civil Service Ministry, the Central Bank of the Republic of Yemen; and the Ministry of Local Government. Coordination was expected at the level of PFM Reform Ministerial Committee chaired by Finance Minister, but such meetings rarely took place. If they did, they were more of a dialogue between MOF and donors rather than exchanges between various ministries. There was a PFM Task Force set up under the chair of Vice Minister Finance to help with more routine issues regarding implementation, but that task force rarely met.

According to the plan, quarterly progress reports accounting for physical and financial progress were to be prepared by the PFMAU for the benefit of donors and the Government. These were also to be presented in the PFM Donor Group meetings in a matrix form comparing the targets with achievements. While the PFMAU did furnish these progress reports occasionally, it was not able to do so on a regular basis.

Staff motivation has been a problem in the Republic of Yemen. The multidonor funded PFMAU is staffed with advisors, accountants, translators and secretaries with monthly salaries that could range as much as 10 times the average salary of US$250 for other civil servants. The PFMAU staff were contractual and committed to work on the reforms, but the major burden of implementation fell upon the shoulders of regular civil servants. They did not have the same motivation unless a particular reform was seen as an immediate priority by the Finance Minister.

The PFM Reforms were not planned to be piloted in certain agencies or departments. They were to strengthen PFM systems that were cross-cutting all ministries. It was the Finance Ministry that was the focus of all reform measures.

From the experience of PFM reform in the Republic of Yemen, one can say reforms that are "self reinforcing"—like the reforms in budget classification or developing a link between the Public Investment Program and Investment Budget—are more successful than those requiring constant inputs and attention, like keeping the aggregate budget out-turn within close proximity to the original approved budget.

While the first phase of PFM reform had modest success, the government has prepared its vision and priorities for Phase 2 of the reform program on the basis of the PEFA assessment and the performance of Phase 1 of the program. The priorities include establishment of a commitment control system and an extension of the AFMIS system. The World Bank intends to support the government in implementing the PFM Reform Strategy. Under the new arrangement, a multidonor trust fund will be set up, with financing from DFID, the Netherlands, and the World Bank. In consultation with these donors, the World Bank is preparing a detailed PFM Reform Action Plan for Phase 2.

Political Economy of Reform

Politics in the Republic of Yemen have historically been dominated by the ruling party, and this has provided some stability for PFM reform. Executive authority has traditionally resided with the President, and it was under his leadership that the National Reforms Agenda (NRA), including PFM reforms, was launched in 2005. The driving force behind the implementation of the NRA is the Deputy Prime Minister (DPM), who has been supportive of this agenda.

The last Parliamentary elections were held in 2003, and the initial term of this Parliament was until April 2009. However, this term has been extended for another two years until April 2011. This has given the government a long period to implement reforms. Elections were held at the governor level in May 2008, in which the Electoral College included only the council members at the district and governorates. Considering the clear majority of ruling General Party Congress (GPC) amongst the council members, the governors-elect were all their nominees. While there has been stability in the Presidency and parliament, there has been less stability at the level of the Minister of Finance and senior levels in the MOF. When the PFM Reform Strategy was approved in 2005, the newly appointed Finance Minister was Dr. Saif Al-Asali. The Minister was strongly supportive of the reform agenda. He drafted several laws, guidelines, and strategies personally, which had the advantage of ownership. Unfortunately, the agenda also became very centralized, which led to a slow-down.

A new Finance Minister, Noaman Al-Sohaibi, was sworn in March 2007. He has also been supportive of PFM reforms and was heavily engaged in the PEFA assessment. Other major accomplishments during his tenure include containing expenditure within the original approved budget of 2007; the publishing of the 2009 budget for public access at the time of its submission to the parliament; linking the investment budget with Public Investment Program in 2008 and 2009; and the introduction of functional classification in the Budget in 2009.

Within the MOF, a new team of Deputy Ministers was appointed in early 2005 largely coming from academia. The complete change of Deputy Ministers at that time does not appear to have helped the reform process. The coordination of reforms within the MOF and with donors was led by the National PFM Coordinator. In March 2008, the position of National PFM Coordinator was upgraded and Mr. Jalal Yaqoub, the Deputy Minister for International Finance Relations in the MOF, was given this responsibility

Key Conclusions

Bringing together the substantive implementation and political analysis, a number of interesting conclusions emerge from the the Republic of Yemen case. The Republic of Yemen has made some progress on PFM reforms where the MOF has put in special effort. This has tended to be where the Finance Minister or the National PFM Coordinator see that the reform can bring instant recognition (such as an improvement in a PEFA indicator) or resources to the government. One example is the enhanced transparency by placing the budget on a website at the time of transmission to parliament. Another is when the MOF introduced functional classification during preparation of the 2009 budget, which was motivated, at least in part, to get a higher PEFA Score.

However, longer term reforms have made less progress in spite of the extensive committee and program management structures that were established. One of the explanations provided is that the officers entrusted with the reforms also have regular duties to perform and are often overloaded with routine work or directed to other tasks by the Finance Minister. It confirms that—while management arrangements may look adequate on paper—they will only be effective if there is a willingness to make them work.

Annex: The Republic of Yemen PEFA Assessment

Table 14A.1. Overview of the Performance Indicator Set

Indicator	MENA Regional PEFA Study 2010	Grade
Credibility of the budget	Aggregate expenditure out-turn compared to original approved budget	D
	Composition of expenditure out-turn compared to original approved budget	C
	Aggregate revenue out-turn compared to original approved budget	A
	Stock and monitoring of expenditure payment arrears	Not Rated
Comprehensiveness and transparency	Classification of the budget	C
	Comprehensiveness of information included in budget documentation	A
	Extent of unreported government operations	B+
	Transparency of intergovernmental fiscal relations	A
	Oversight of aggregate fiscal risk from other public sector entities	A
	Public access to key fiscal information	C
Policy-based budgeting	Orderliness and participation in the annual budget process	A
	Multiyear perspective in fiscal planning, expenditure policy, and budgeting	C+
Predictability and control in budget execution	Transparency of taxpayer obligations and liabilities	B
	Effectiveness of measures for taxpayer registration and tax assessment	B
	Effectiveness in collection of tax payments	D+
	Predictability in the availability of funds for commitment of expenditures	D+
	Recording and management of cash balances, debt, and guarantees	B+
	Effectiveness of payroll controls	D+
	Competition, value for money, and controls in procurement	D+
	Effectiveness of internal controls for nonsalary expenditure	D+
	Effectiveness of internal audit	D+
Accounting, recording, and reporting	Timeliness and regularity of accounts reconciliation	B
	Availability of information on resources received by service delivery units	B
	Quality and timeliness of in-year budget reports	D+
	Quality and timeliness of annual financial statements	C+
External scrutiny and audit	Scope, nature, and follow-up of external audit	B+
	Legislative scrutiny of the annual budget law	C+
	Legislative scrutiny of external audit reports	D+
Donor practices	Predictability of direct budget support	Not Rated
	Financial information provided by donors for budgeting and reporting on project and program aid	Not Rated
	Proportion of aid that is managed by use of national procedures	Not Rated

Source: World Bank.

Notes

1. This is in spite of substantial tax reforms since 2001, including a shift to a self assessment basis and improved customs systems, which have translated into healthier tax revenue streams.

2. They include the Committee on Functional Classification, the Committee on the Accounting Manual, the Committee on the Treasury System, the Committee on Cash Management, the Committee on Internal Audit, and the Committee on Institutional Restructuring and Capacity Building.

Appendix

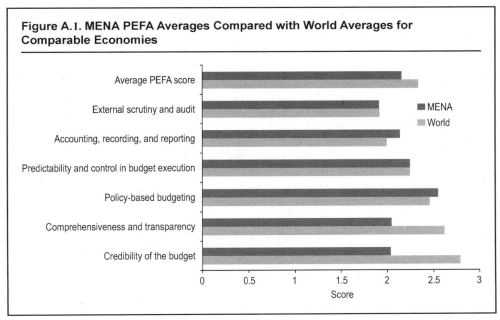

Figure A.1. MENA PEFA Averages Compared with World Averages for Comparable Economies

Source: World Bank.

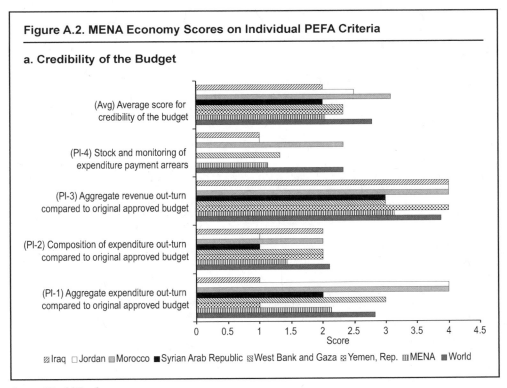

Figure A.2. MENA Economy Scores on Individual PEFA Criteria

a. Credibility of the Budget

Source: World Bank.

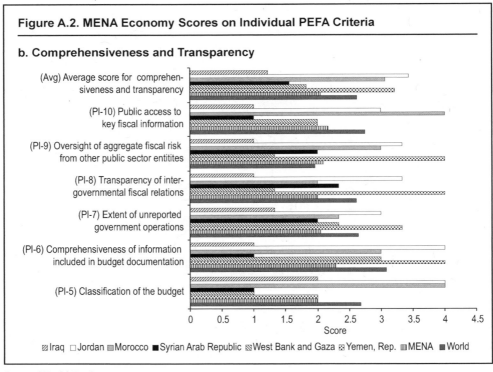

Source: World Bank.

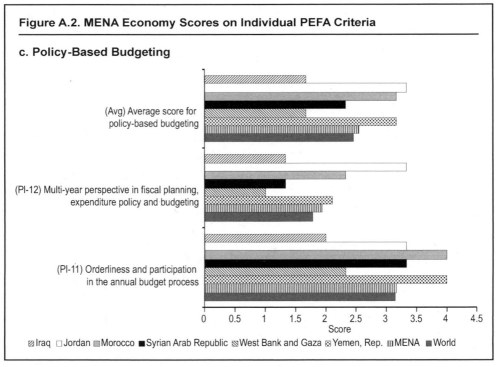

Source: World Bank.

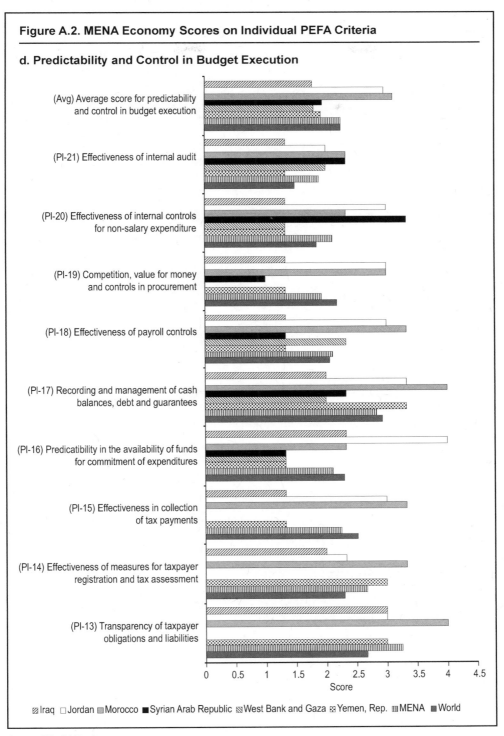

Figure A.2. MENA Economy Scores on Individual PEFA Criteria

d. Predictability and Control in Budget Execution

(Avg) Average score for predictability and control in budget execution

(PI-21) Effectiveness of internal audit

(PI-20) Effectiveness of internal controls for non-salary expenditure

(PI-19) Competition, value for money and controls in procurement

(PI-18) Effectiveness of payroll controls

(PI-17) Recording and management of cash balances, debt and guarantees

(PI-16) Predicatibility in the availability of funds for commitment of expenditures

(PI-15) Effectiveness in collection of tax payments

(PI-14) Effectiveness of measures for taxpayer registration and tax assessment

(PI-13) Transparency of taxpayer obligations and liabilities

Score

0   0.5   1   1.5   2   2.5   3   3.5   4   4.5

Iraq Jordan Morocco Syrian Arab Republic West Bank and Gaza Yemen, Rep. MENA World

Source: World Bank.

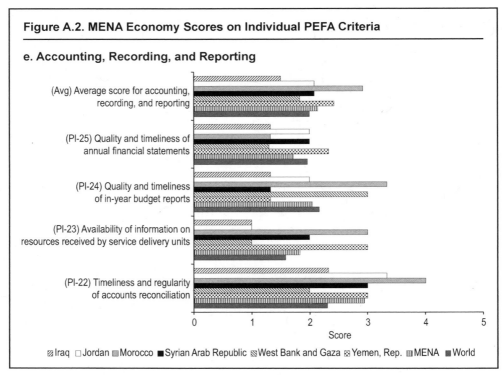

Figure A.2. MENA Economy Scores on Individual PEFA Criteria

e. Accounting, Recording, and Reporting

Source: World Bank.

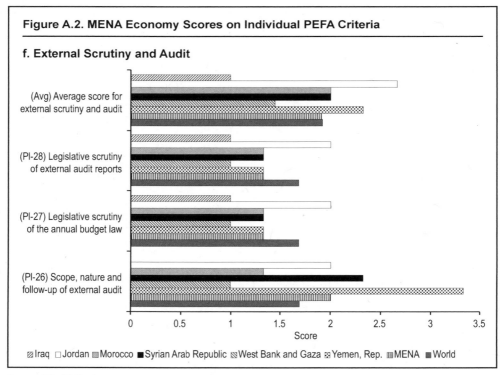

Figure A.2. MENA Economy Scores on Individual PEFA Criteria

f. External Scrutiny and Audit

Source: World Bank.

Bibliography

General Sources

Andrews, M. 2008. "PFM in Africa: Where Are We, How Did We Get Here, Where Should We Go? Lessons from Recent PEFA Data and World Bank Public Financial Management Performance Reports." Research study for Brookings Institution and World Bank.

de Renzio, P. 2009. "What do PEFA Assessments Tell Us about PFM Reforms across Countries?" Working Paper No. 302. Overseas Development Institute.

Global Integrity. 2009. *Global Integrity Index*. Washington, DC: Global Integrity.

International Country Risk Guide. 2009. *ICRG Corruption Index*. www.prsgroup.com/icrg.

International Finance Corporation (IFC). 2010. *Doing Business: Measuring Business Regulations—Tunisia*. Washington, DC: IFC.

Pretorius, C., and N. Pertorius. 2009. *Review of Public Financial Management Reform Literature*. Evaluation Report EV698. London: United Kingdom Department for International Development Evaluation.

Transparency International. 2009. *Corruption Perceptions Index*. Berlin: Transparency International.

World Bank. 2008. *Public Sector Reform: What Works and Why?* Washington, DC: World Bank.

———. 2009. *Global Corruption Barometer Report*. Berlin: Transparency International.

Algeria

International Monetary Fund (IMF). 2005. *Algeria Report on the Observance of Standards and Codes (ROSC) Fiscal Transparency Module*. IMF Country Report No. 05/68. Washington, DC: IMF.

World Bank. 2007. *People's Democratic Republic of Algeria Public Expenditure Review (PER): Assuring High Quality Public Investment*. World Bank Report No. 36270-DZ. Washington, DC: World Bank.

———. 2009. *Budget Systems Modernization Project Implementation Completion and Results Report (ICR)*. World Bank Report No. ICR1130. Washington, DC: World Bank.

Egypt

Author interview. 2009a. H.E. Youssef Boutros Ghali, November.

———. 2009b. H.E. Youssef Boutros Ghali, Ashraf Gamal El-Din, Gamil Ezzat and Ayhmed Monkez Shaker, Egyptian Tax Authority, 2009.

Bodin, J. P., Olivier Benon, and Chaouki Hamad. 2008. *Egypt Modernizing Tax Administration—Current Status and Next Steps*. Washington, DC: IMF.

European Commission. 2009. *Egypt PEFA Assessment (DRAFT)*. Paris: The European Commission.

International Monetary Fund (IMF). 2005. *Enhancing Treasury and Budget Reforms*. Washington, DC: IMF.

———. 2006. *Modernizing the Property Tax: Agricultural Land Tax*. Washington, DC: IMF.

———. 2007. *Fiscal Reporting: Strengthening the Accounting, Consolidation and Reconciliation Frameworks*, Washington, DC: IMF.

———. 2009. *Reviving Momentum of TSA and Related Reforms (DRAFT)*. Washington, DC: IMF.

Nagarajan, Nithya. 2010. *Egypt: Overhaul of Tax Policy and Administration*. MENA Governance Case Program. World Bank and Dubai School of Government

Ramalho, Rita. 2008. *Adding a Million Taxpayers*. Doing Business survey. Washington, DC: World Bank.

World Bank. 2005. *Public Expenditure Review—Policy Note 6, Budget Construction and Decentralization*. Washington, DC: The World Bank.

———. 2008. *Egypt Country Financial Accountability Assessment*. Washington, DC: World Bank.

———. 2009. "Egypt Country Governance Brief." World Bank, Washington, DC.

Iraq

Government of Iraq. 2007. *International Compact with Iraq and accompanying Joint Monitoring Matrix*. Baghdad.

———. 2008. *Public Financial Management Reform Strategy*. July. Baghdad.

IMF. 2005. *Budget Classification Reform*. Washington, DC: IMF.

———. 2007. *Issues in Tax Reform*. Washington, DC: IMF.

———. 2008. *Reform Priorities in Public Financial Management*. Washington, DC: IMF.

United States Agency for International Development (USAID). 2009. *Iraq Financial Management Information System Assessment*. Washington, DC: USAID. http://pdf.usaid.gov/pdf_docs/PNADO270.pdf.

World Bank. 2008a. *Iraq Public Expenditure and Institutional Assessment (PEIA) Volume 1: Public Financial Management in a Conflict-Affected Environment*. Washington, DC: World Bank.

———. 2008b. *Iraq Public Expenditure and Institutional Assessment (PEIA) Volume 2: Public Expenditure and Financial Accountability (PEFA) Assessment Public*. Washington, DC: World Bank.

———. 2009. "Iraq Country Governance Brief." World Bank, Washington, DC.

Financial Management Report. Internal Bank document. Washington, DC: World Bank.

World Bank and IMF. 2005. *Enhancing Sound Public Financial Management: Short to Medium-Term Reforms*. Washington, DC: World Bank and IMF.

Jordan

European Commission (EC). 2007. *Jordan Public Expenditure Financial Assessment*. Paris: EC.

Government of Jordan. Ministry of Finance website, available at www.mof.gov.jo.

———. *Ministry of Finance: Strategy for 2005–2009 and 2008–2010*. Amman.

———. 2007a. *Financial Management Reform Strategy 2004–2007*. Ministry of Finance. Amman.

———. 2007b. *General Budget Department's Strategy for 2007–2009*. Amman.

———. n.d. *Cabinet Office Policy Statement for Public Sector Reform*. Amman.

International Monetary Fund (IMF). 2005. *Tax Administration Integration and Modernization*. Washington, DC: IMF.

———. 2006a. *Aide Memoire: Jordan Treasury Single Account and Supporting Measures – Review of Progress*. Washington, DC: IMF.

———. 2006b. *Technical Assistance in Tax Administration*. Washington, DC: IMF.

———. 2008. *Treasury Single Account and Measures for Further Strengthening of Cash Management*. Washington, DC: IMF.

Nagarajan, N. "Cabinet Decision Support Reforms: The Case of Jordan" Case Study 2009–01. World Bank and Dubai School of Government (forthcoming).

World Bank. 2006. *Aide Memoire: Jordan Public Expenditure Review—Technical Assistance Mission*. World Bank, Washington, DC.

———. 2008a. *Aide Memoire: Jordan Public Expenditure Review—Technical Assistance Mission*. World Bank, Washington, DC.

———. 2008b. "Jordan Country Governance Brief." World Bank, Washington, DC.

———. 2008c. "Public Financial Management Background Note (DRAFT)." World Bank, Washington, DC.

———. 2009. *Progress Assessment in Introducing a Medium Term Expenditure Framework*. Washington, DC: The World Bank.

World Bank and IMF. 2004. *Work Program for Consolidating Budget Management Reforms*. Washington, DC: World Bank and IMF.

———. 2009. *Jordan: Advancing the PFM Reform Agenda*. Washington, DC: World Bank and IMF.

Lebanon

Government of Lebanon. 2007. *Reforms at the Ministry of Finance, A Clear Vision Leading the Way, 2005–2007 and Beyond*. Beirut: Ministry of Finance.

International Monetary Fund (IMF). 2005. *Lebanon: Report on Observance of Standards and Codes-Fiscal Transparency Module*. Washington, DC: IMF.

———. 2007. *Lebanon: Improving Cash Management*. Washington, DC: IMF.

———. 2008. *Lebanon: Improving Cash Management*. Washington, DC: IMF.

———. 2009. *Lebanon: 2009 Article IV Consultation Mission, Mission Concluding Statement*. Washington, DC: IMF.

Nahas, C. 2009. *Understanding Resilience: The Skills Needed and the Costs Incurred, Political Economy of the Lebanese System (1985–2005)*. Washington, DC: World Bank.

World Bank. 2005. *Lebanon Country Financial Accountability Assessment (CFAA)*. Washington, DC: World Bank.

———. 2007. *Terms of Reference for the IDF Grant to the Institute of Finance of Lebanon for Developing Capacity Building Tools for Sustainable Governance in Lebanon and the MENA Region*. Washington, DC: World Bank.

———. 2008a. *EFMIS Project Document*. Washington, DC: World Bank.

———. 2008b. "Lebanon Country Governance Brief." World Bank, Washington, DC.

Morocco

International Monetary Fund (IMF). 2005. *Morocco: Report on Observance of Standards and Codes—Fiscal Transparency Module.* IMF Country Report No. 05/298. Washington, DC: IMF.

World Bank. 2003. *Morocco Country Financial Accountability Assessment (CFAA).* Washington, DC: World Bank.

———. 2007. *Morocco Country Financial Accountability Assessment (CFAA).* Washington, DC: World Bank.

World Bank and European Commission. 2009. *Public Financial Management Performance Report (PEFA)—Assessment of Public Financial Management Systems, Procedures, and Institutions.* Washington, DC: World Bank.

The Syrian Arab Republic

European Commission (EC). 2008. *Formulation of the Public Finance Reform Program.* Paris: EC.

International Monetary Fund (IMF). 2007a. *Syria: Accelerating the Tax Administration Reforms and Preparations for the VAT.* Washington, DC: IMF.

———. 2007b. *Syria: Budget Modernization.* Washington, DC: IMF.

———. 2008. *Syria: Implementing Budget Modernization.* Washington, DC: IMF.

World Bank. 2008. *Aide Memoire of CPAR Scoping Mission.* Washington, DC: World Bank.

World Bank/IMF. 2006. *Syria—Public Financial Management Report.* Washington, DC: World Bank and IMF.

Tunisia

Government of Tunisia. 2007. *XIth Development Plan (2007–2011).* Tunisia: Country Regional Department. Tunis.

———. 2010. *Tunisia 2010–2014 Development Plan.* Tunis.

Schiavo Campo, S. 2008. *Tunisia Development Policy Review.* Washington, DC: World Bank.

World Bank. 2004. *Tunisia Country Financial Accountability Assessment (CFAA).* Washington, DC: World Bank.

———. 2008. *Tunisia Country Governance Brief.* Washington, DC: World Bank.

The West Bank and Gaza

Ernst and Young/Ministry of Finance. 2008. *Systems Functionality Review Report.* Palestine: Ernst and Young/Ministry of Finance.

European Union (EU). 2008. *Needs Assessment and Project Identification for SAACB.* Jerusalem: EU.

Fayyad, P. 2008. Transcript. (R. Khouri, Interviewer). October.

International Monetary Fund (IMF). 2009. *Advancing Public Financial Management Reforms.* Washington, DC: IMF.

———. 2007. *Public Financial Management System: Immediate Challenges and Medium-Term Issues.* Washington, DC: IMF.

———. 2008a. *Functional Analysis of Public Financial Management Processes and Interface with the Palestine Government Accounting System.* Beirut, Lebanon: IMF.

————. 2008b. *Improvements in the Palestine Government Accounting System and Updating of the Financial Regulations*. Beirut, Lebanon: IMF.

————. 2008c. *Public Financial Management Reform*. Washington, DC: IMF.

Nagarajan, N. 2007. Interview with Prime Minister Salam Fayyad, November.

————. 2008. *Case Studies in Governance and Public Management in the Middle East and North Africa: Reforms to Public Financial Management in Palestine*. Washington, DC: World Bank and Dubai School of Government.

Palestinian National Authority. 2008. *Palestinian Reform and Development Plan*.

World Bank. 2004. *West Bank and Gaza Country Financial Accountability Assessment (CFAA)*. Washington, DC: World Bank.

————. 2007. *Public Expenditure Review*. Washington, DC: World Bank.

The Republic of Yemen

Government of Yemen.2007. *Yemen Medium-Term National Development Framework. (DPPR)*. Sana'a.

United Nations Development Programme (UNDP) and Government of Yemen. 2006. *Implementation of Public Financial Management Reform Action Plan*. UNDP and Government of Yemen.

World Bank. 2003. *Yemen Country Procurement Assessment Report*. Washington, DC: World Bank.

————. 2004. *Yemen Country Financial Accountability Assessment (CFAA)*. Washington, DC: World Bank.

————. 2005. *Tracking Basic Education Expenditures in Yemen: Analyses of Public Resource Management and Teacher Absenteeism*. Washington, DC: World Bank

————. 2008. *Republic of Yemen Public Expenditure and Financial Accountability Assessment (PEFA)*. Washington, DC: World Bank, July.

ECO-AUDIT
Environmental Benefits Statement

The World Bank is committed to preserving endangered forests and natural resources. The Office of the Publisher has chosen to print World Bank Studies and Working Papers on recycled paper with 30 percent postconsumer fiber in accordance with the recommended standards for paper usage set by the Green Press Initiative, a non-profit program supporting publishers in using fiber that is not sourced from endangered forests. For more information, visit www.greenpressinitiative.org.

In 2010, the printing of this book on recycled paper saved the following:

- 11 trees*
- 3 million Btu of total energy
- 1,045 lb. of net greenhouse gases
- 5,035 gal. of waste water
- 306 lb. of solid waste

* 40 feet in height and 6–8 inches in diameter